# A Mental Note

I0118143

# William Roberts

**chipmunkapublishing**
the mental health publisher

Published by
Chipmunkapublishing
PO Box 6872
Brentwood
Essex CM13 1ZT
United Kingdom

**http://www.chipmunkapublishing.com**

ISBN    978-1-84991-650-9

Chipmunkapublishing gratefully acknowledge the support of Arts Council England.

## Author Biography

William is a man with a story of courage. He was born in Shrewsbury, Shropshire UK in 1980. He was educated privately in Shrewsbury, and at Adams School, Newport, Shropshire, where he achieved 8 healthy GCSEs. Trouble set in in his mid-teens when he was caught between the Sixth Form College, Shrewsbury, and the Radbrook College, Shrewsbury, where he transferred from an academic to a practical career prospect, studying to be a chef. From Shrewsbury to Croydon near London he pursued his chef career. He had a breakdown, out of which he has pulled himself together, and written 'A MENTAL NOTE' – an imaginative and dynamic fictional testimony to what it is to be like to be pained by schizophrenia, but to work one's way through. He is currently living in Birmingham, and writing his next, imaginative books.

A Mental Note

# CHAPTER 1

## Episode One

October 5, 2006. It's a pretty cold day. Not bad for the time of year I suppose – could be warmer though. I bet Mum's warmer. She's somewhere across the Med on a cruise ship with her husband. Thirteen floors apparently! Three theatres, Lord knows how many restaurants, and a casino.

Hmmm, a casino. That's where I'd be, if I had any money. Not Mum though, gambling didn't appeal to Mum. Apart from being too sensible and knowing that the house always wins, she probably wouldn't understand how to play anyway.

I do seem to remember playing blackjack with her when I was younger. Only for matchsticks though – you know – for fun.

Yeah, Mum will probably be in one of the restaurants trying out the various cuisines on offer, or catching a show in one of the three theatres (how many theatres does a boat need?) Sounds all very glamorous. Not my idea of a good holiday though: stuck on a ship with nothing to see but water.

Still, each to their own and after all it is her birthday. Oh didn't I mention, that's right, today she is sixty-eight and this was Eric's (that's her husband) treat for nearly reaching the golden age of seventy. Probably not his idea of a good holiday either, but you know, 'whatever the lady desires' and all that. Fair play to him that's what I say.

I would phone to wish her a happy birthday but their phones don't work so far from the shore. I'd let her know that everything's okay and tell her not to worry. I'd tell her to watch Eric and that casino, not that he knows how to play anything there anyway. I'd warn her not to go to crazy on the food in all those restaurants, but most importantly, I'd say to her: "However much Eric winds you up – DON'T throw him overboard!" Oh well, I'm sure she won't.

"Happy birthday, Mum. Hope you're okay – I'm fine. Say hi to Eric for me, and I'll see you soon, okay."

Yeah, Eric's a good bloke. We'd had our fallouts in the past but he looked after my mum and for that, I cannot fault him. Right plonker though – into his crown green bowling. In fact, he's captain of the local club's B-team. On occasion, Mum and I used to go down to watch him play when there was a home game. Eric thought we were there to support his team: we were really there to take the Mick out of him, and to take advantage of the incredibly cheap bar.

"Good wood sir – jolly good wood indeed," we would shout from the sideline, trying not to laugh, as I held a pint in my hand, while Mum stood next to me, dipping her ready-salted crisps into her tomato juice.

When it was Eric's turn to bowl – that was the real highlight. He would line up his shot, take a back swing and release the bowl (just like everyone else really), but if his bowl looked wide, he would perform this hand gesture as if he was stroking an invisible dog. I think it was to somehow try and magically steer the ball back to its target. The wider the bowl – the bigger the dog: it was a joy to watch, had us in tears.

"Another drink, Mum?"

"Jolly good idea, Sir."

Yeah, Stella (that's my mum by the way) and Eric had been together for years. Lost count exactly how many, yet I do know they'd been married for four of them. I remember the wedding – it was great. I can picture mum wearing that stunning gold dress; her hair styled beautifully. All of her friends and family were there for her big day - I mean the place was packed.

Then there was Eric. Eric was dressed top to toe in this dark green suit, looking more like a tennis umpire than the groom, but if you think that's bad, you should have heard his speech. Something along the lines of 'never wearing ladies underwear,' I won't go into that now though.

You know the best thing about mum's wedding – the best thing, was shaking Marcus' hand after the service and calling him 'brother.' Marcus is Eric's youngest son and we get on like a house on fire: he's so funny.

I remember once we went down to Eric's bowls club and had a bit of a (hmmm) practice on the green. Marcus got banned for life for taking out some poor guys legs with a – shall we say – slightly over the top smash shot. The thing was there were no other balls to smash! Luckily the manager didn't realize that it was Eric's son. That would have made for a whole world of messy sugar, but as it happened there was no harm done (apart from the geezer's legs of course).

Even before mum got married we considered ourselves brothers, but now it was official.

After the wedding service and a few words with some of the guests, we all sat down for the meal: a choice of either pork or fish. Either side of me at the dinner table were Marcus and Chris (that's my sister-in-law), Christine to be exact. Now trust me when I tell you that, boy, can she can go on, and on, and on:

"Don't you think you've had enough Champagne, William?" and; "I don't think you should drink any more Champagne, William!" and; "You really should make that your last glass of Champagne, William," and so on.

"Okay okay, I will I will. Hey Mum, thanks for the meal, the pork was sublime. Come on Marcus, let's find the bar."

There was a very good reason why Chris went on, especially at me. She was worried about me. In fact, a lot of people were worried about me, including my mum – especially my mum.

Chris was married to my older brother Ben. He was my real brother, but the fact that he lived nearly two-hundred miles away meant that I didn't see him much. Usually round Christmas time or special occasions; mums wedding for example – stuff like that.

He's a good bloke though: bit of a workaholic. He's got his own landscaping business down in Berkshire. He does a lot of tree surgery, things like that. Great place to set up, Berkshire, it's full of bloody trees (clever boy). It's paid off though. He owns a great big house in Ascot, nice cars and loads of money. Trouble is, he doesn't have any free time to spend it as he's always working. Still, whatever floats your boat, and when your boat's as big as his, it takes hard work to keep it afloat.

Yeah, despite the long distance between us, we're still close. I just wish he wouldn't worry so much. Honestly – I'm fine.

Then there's Jolie my girlfriend – no, sorry – fiancée. Oh hang on a second – no, girlfriend, I was right the first time. We did get engaged but now we're not. It's nothing to worry about, just a spot of turbulence in our crazy relationship. Everything's fine now, I just haven't proposed again (successfully) – yet.

Well now, what can I say about Jolie. She's just brilliant; I love her to bits. We live together in this weird three-storey house on a pretty grim street in quite a desirable area of Shrewsbury. To be honest it's pretty horrid, but it sounds quite impressive when you describe it to people.

The other member of our household is little Matty, Jolie's son. He's at the troublesome age of two-and-a-half, and I've got to be honest, troublesome is definitely the correct description; he can really be a pain in the backside, but in all fairness, he's great, just a handful that's all. But then what kid isn't?

Still, better get used to it because in roughly eight weeks, there's going to be another one; little girl this time. Jolie insisted on paying for the scan to find out with this one. She says it's so you can be more prepared: I think she was just getting fed up with buying cream clothes all the time. Still, it does mean you can think about a name: haven't got a clue what we're going to call her though. Maybe wait till the baby comes and decide then.

"Yeah, that's a good idea Will, wait till she's born. Then you can see what she looks like. What a good idea."

I've got lots of good ideas floating around my head. Here's just a few -

1. Foot odour powder in various fruit flavors.
2. A remote controlled indoor TV aerial.
3. A new magnetic energy source.
4. A new alcopop called 'Quack Daniels'.
5. An annual wildebeest chase – to be held at the Quarry in Shrewsbury.
6. No wait Will: don't give too many away – that's a good idea.

Anyway, it's starting to get a bit cold in here.

"Why don't you put a jumper on; that's a good idea."

Today is Mum's birthday, and I've spent the last three hours sitting on my bed, staring out of the window. I'm not sure what I've been staring at exactly, but I do know that the view's great from the third floor. It's sort of like a penthouse, apart from the fact that the two floors below are ours too.

Still, the top floor is definitely my favorite. It's where I feel safe when no one else is home. It's also where I paint my pictures.

Oh, did I not mention, yeah, I'm a bit of an artist in my free time. I use soft pastels to create – you could say – abstract and sometimes minimal art, incorporating swirls and smudges using bold, bright colors. I like the slightly more expensive pastels as they leave more of a creamy texture. Definitely worth the extra money. I'm not too sure what the pictures are supposed to be, or what they will look like before I start, but nevertheless, people seem to like them. Maybe people think they're weird and wonder what's going on inside my head to draw them.

Ha – wouldn't I like to know?

Not too many people know about the voices in my head. Ah yes, the voices, the bloody voices. What have I got to say about those damned things. Well, for me they're everywhere – and they're nowhere. They have no face and they have no name. They must have a purpose but really, most of the time they just get on my nerves. I hear them in the leaves blowing in the trees; the clock ticking on the wall; the kettle boiling and that noisy hand dryer in the gent's toilet. I can even hear them when I'm running a bath, I mean, do they have no respect!

I can't say too many bad things about them though. In my eyes they had done me a favor once. In fact it was more that a favor; you could say that I owed them my life. That was a while ago, and now I just wanted to know who they were, so I could thank them personally and get on with the rest of my days.

I've been searching for that answer for years now, still with no clue. Why this was happening I do not know. Why me? Who's trying to communicate with me? When is it going to stop? What is going on? I'm still not sure of any of this, but remember, it's only October 5, 2006. What I do know, is that it was the voices that changed everything, but for that story – you have to go back.

It all started six years ago. I had a live-in job in Croydon (Surrey) working as a grill chef in a busy restaurant called *The Lodge*. The manager was this stocky Italian guy called Cioffi. Rumour had it that you never saw him before lunchtime because he took so many steroids, and found it almost impossible to get out of bed.

He used to patrol the restaurant floor in one of his Armani suits, shrugging his shoulders and jolting his neck back and forth like some sort of wingless pigeon. It did look a bit strange and we did take the Mick, but to be fair, you couldn't wish for a better boss – he was a star.

"Hey boys," he'd say in a real rough, robotic tone, "are we doing the business or what?"

"Of course we are Cioffi; of course we are."

"Hey Will. What do you think of these new bread rolls we're getting in for the soup?"

"Oh they're the business Cioffi; the business," I'd reply.

"That's right Will. They're the business; the bloody business."

Cioffi liked me for some reason. He used to call me a 'likeable rogue' and 'a stick in the mud'. He didn't like me to start with though, especially considering that when he arrived back from a month's break at his holiday home in Florida, he came in to find that I'd been employed and was using his office as a bedroom.

After a while, however, I grew on him, and besides – I was a good chef. More importantly: I was a fast chef. And when you're grilling for three hundred people every night – you have to be fast to keep up. It was a tough job to say the least.

I am still a good chef though: wouldn't do it for a living again – all that grease and sweat – no thanks. At the time it was great. I was best mates with one of the other chefs called Toby (or as I liked to call him – Captain). He was slightly older than I was, with short, spiky blonde hair: cheeky chappy: real ladies man. I mean, at the time he was dating the most gorgeous waitress in the restaurant. All the boys were envious of Toby – he had it made.

The trouble was, he couldn't cook to save his life. I remember the first time we did breakfast together. I asked him to cook a boiled egg and the silly sod went and stuck it under the grill! It didn't matter to me though – he was a laugh. We always did have a laugh, so after a few months of knowing each other, we decided to save up and get our own place. It was perfect.

For the next six months we saved up our pennies whilst looking for somewhere affordable to rent. I can remember the anticipation nearly killing me. The time soon passed however and just over half a year later – we had done it. Our great idea was to be a reality. Cioffi was happy too, I think. He could finally have the office to himself, and shift that camping bed which was propped up against his desk.

We moved into a two-bedroom ground floor flat, just a short tram journey from the restaurant. It was great, but to be honest – anything would have been adequate. Toby got the big room (after all – he was the Captain), and I got the box room at the end of the hall with the single bed. That was fine by me. Most nights, I would end up falling asleep in the sitting room watching TV anyway.

The only annoying thing really, was that when it came to washing the dishes – there was no hot water in the kitchen. The landlord didn't seem to show much of an interest in the place (apart from the last Friday of every month, he tended to grace us with his presence on those particular days), so we had to boil the kettle, or fill the washing-up basin from the shower, which took forever. This was unnecessary time consumption for us though. We liked to use our time for more meaningful activities, such as – going out on the town and getting plastered, or sitting at home watching repeat episodes of '*Only Fools and Horses*' and '*The Simpsons*'. At the end of the day we worked hard – so why not? We were happy: I was happy; in fact you could say that I was on top of the world; nothing could touch me (or so I thought).

When you're sitting on top of the world, it's a long way down. On a cloudy day, you can't even see the bottom. Now on this particular day, it was thick fog, and was to be the day that things were about to get very different. There was no way of preparing myself for the following chain of events, plus I don't even know if there was any way of preventing them, it all just happened.

My descent was rapid. At first, I thought it was people living upstairs playing a joke on me, I even thought Toby could have been involved. I could hear voices, which at the time seemed to be coming from or through the ceiling. I heard laughing, and people teasing me as if they were watching or listening to me somehow. The possibility that Toby had made friends with the neighbours, and had set up cameras or microphones in our flat crossed my mind.

When Toby got back from work that day, I questioned him about it, and told him what I thought was going on. He just looked at me as if I was crazy though. Nevertheless, I hunted the flat for cameras. I even unscrewed the plug sockets and ripped chunks away from the wallpaper in desperate hope of finding something – but I couldn't.

That night – I did not sleep.

The next day, things got worse. I was due on the lunch shift at twelve. Toby had already gone to work early to do the breakfast shift, so I was alone. I was tired from the lack of sleep, yet I felt good that I would be getting out of the flat.

I could still hear voices as I rushed to get ready for work, and at about half-past-eleven, I grabbed my jacket and left the flat. I'd barely reached half way up the road towards the tram stop, when I suddenly stopped in my tracks and listened: people were shouting – shouting at me. I looked around but nobody was in sight. I carried on walking but the voices got louder. I could barely make out what they were saying but knew it wasn't nice. I froze; looked around again – still no one there. I panicked. I could see the tram stop, but my instinct was to get indoors, so I turned around and quickly marched back to the flat.

It was rapidly becoming clear that this was no joke – someone had it in for me. I thought I'd find sanctuary back at home but the voices were still there. I locked myself in the bathroom and turned off the light to try and somehow hide from whoever was doing this to me – there was no escape.

Everywhere I went; whatever I did – I could hear the voices. They were saying things like 'Get out and don't come back or you're dead' (to put it politely). I didn't know what to do. There was nobody about who could help, and also I was afraid that people were going to come and (literally) kill me.

After about half an hour of trying to think straight, I decided that getting out, there and then, was the only option. I phoned my mum who was back in Shrewsbury and told her what was going on, and that I needed to come home – ASAP.

I packed some bits and pieces in a hysterical frenzy and left the flat. Hastily I walked towards the tram stop, constantly looking over my shoulder, convinced someone was going to run up behind and attack me, but they never did.

I boarded the tram on the other side of the station from where I usually did. This time I was heading for the train station to catch a train back to Shrewsbury. It was to be a long journey. It was quite a distance anyway, but this time it felt even longer. I was leaving my job, my best friend and my house behind, knowing that I wasn't going back.

I never rang work to tell them what had happened, I mean – what was I supposed to say? I never rang Toby either. I just hoped he was going to be able to cope with the rent without me.

Cioffi would be disappointed in me. The feeling of guilt flowed through my skin, mixed with the uncontrollable urge to vomit. The rocking motion of the train wasn't helping either; nor had the voices gone. The constant roar as the train shot through the countryside just seemed to magnify them, as I sat – scared in my seat; my eyes glued to the window, desperately avoiding contact with anyone – but I didn't vomit.

As the train pulled into Shrewsbury station, there, standing on the platform waiting for me, was (an anxious-looking) Mum. I was so glad to see her. I don't think I've ever felt that relieved in my entire life.

As we reached a standstill, I headed for the door. I nearly got stuck as I urgently tried to get off the train with whatever belongings I'd remembered to bring with me. That didn't matter now though. What did matter was that I felt safe, knowing mum was going to take care of me. I didn't say much at the time – just gave her a hug, headed for the car park, and drove home.

That evening we talked as I tried to explain everything. My story just confused her, but there was no way of explaining it any more clearly. I was confused myself, but these voices were real. They were a lot fainter by then but nevertheless, I could tell they were still there.

Mum seemed concerned and suggested it would be wise to have an early night. I agreed, so shortly after talking – I went to bed. Downstairs you could hear Mum and Eric discussing the situation at great length. They must have thought I was going mad.

"I haven't gone mad have I Will? Nah can't be: this is real, isn't it? Of course it's real, I can hear the voices – or is that just Mum and Eric? Don't know. You're not mad though Will – definitely not mad. Mind you, you are talking to yourself, but that's okay. Get some sleep now all right: goodnight."

It was clear to me the next morning what conclusion Mum and Eric had reached, because by lunchtime the psychiatrist had arrived. I had calmed down a lot by then and was ready to talk (for all the good it would do). It was a warm day and I was sitting in the conservatory with the dog. She was a King Charles Spaniel called Tilly, and had recently given birth to puppies, three in all, if I recall correctly.

I sat at the table with a cup of strong coffee under the overhead fan, gazing at the garden and stroking the dog. Suddenly the conservatory door swung open. Mum came through, followed by this Indian guy in a grey suit, carrying a briefcase.

"Hello, William. My name is Doctor Shizad, and I'm a psychiatrist," he said.

"Hi," I replied, thinking to myself that this was such a big waste of time.

"I'm just going to check on the pups," said Mum as she left the conservatory, shutting the door softly behind her.

All of a sudden, I felt nervous again. The doctor sat down and unbuckled the clips of his leather briefcase. He pulled out some paperwork and put on his spectacles.

"Now then, William, your mother has informed me that you've been having a few problems. Is that correct?" he asked.

"You could say that," I replied.

"Okay then, what I'd like to do is ask you some questions, and I just want you to do your best to answer them. Would that be okay?"

"Fine," I said.

He pulled out a silver fountain pen from his inside pocket and proceeded with the interview.

Two coffees later and the interrogation was over.

Mum came through for the verdict.

"Paranoid schizophrenia," he concluded.

"Paranoid what?" I said.

"Schizophrenia," he repeated, and then proceeded to inform me what it all meant.

Basically, the general picture was this – there was a chemical imbalance in my brain, which triggers hallucinations (in this case – voices). Any number of reasons could have caused it to occur, but there was no test or scan to actually prove that this was the case.

I was having none of it.

"It can't be schizophrenia – I've never been paranoid," I argued. "And these voices are real: I should know – I can hear them."

"Okay then, William: so where exactly are these voices coming from?" he asked.

I paused for a moment, trying to think of an explanation, but could find no logical answer to give. Instead, all I could do was shrug my shoulders. The doctor then turned to Mum and started to explain things more deeply, while I sat back in my chair, gazing out of the window in disbelief. No way had I imagined all of this – no way.

"Here – these tablets should help control the voices, William," he said, as he wrote out a prescription with his silver pen.

He presented me with the green piece of paper. I vaguely glanced at it but just scrumpled it up and shoved it in my jeans pocket: a disgruntled look across my face. Then Mum took the doctor through to the kitchen to discuss matters in private, whilst I sat in my chair with my head down, hypnotised by the bottom of my empty cup of coffee.

I could faintly make out their discussion. I couldn't believe that mum was buying all that talk about chemical imbalances and what have you. I was angry with her for not believing me, and believing him – this stupid man who didn't even know me.

I slammed down my coffee cup, and burst into the kitchen.

"As you're here, Professor Smart-Ass, why don't you check on the puppies, and make sure they're not barking mad too!"

Before I could get a response, I stormed up the stairs to my room and shut the door, wishing to speak to no one. But people were speaking to me: I could hear them. I was not sure who they were, but I was sure they were real – that much was true.

Despite believing this, I reached into my pocket, pulled out the prescription and straightened it out against my thigh. I couldn't even pronounce what the tablets were called, yet, after another coffee and a brief chat with Mum, I promised to give them a go. However, I made 'a mental note' – this was real!

It's been just over six years now, and I still refuse to accept that this is my illness. The tablets just make me tired, so I compromise, and take half (sometimes – maybe). The voices are still here – they've never gone away, but I've found happiness again. I am living with the girl I love: I've got new friends, and my favourite pastime – painting.

I've come to realise that despite what I hear, nothing really bad ever happens. I have developed tolerance for the voices, and I've found that painting is a good means of channelling my attention.

It's October 5, 2006, and in just over eight weeks there will be something else to focus my mind on. It's going to be great: a little Will to look after – can't wait. Perhaps that's why I've spent the last three hours staring out of the window, thinking about becoming a dad. Or maybe I'm wondering what to cook for dinner tonight: I'm staring into space, thinking about nothing at all. I'm not too sure now – I can't remember.

"Blimey, it's cold in here: where's that jumper?"

"Oh, and Happy Birthday, Mum! Don't worry – I'm fine."

## CHAPTER 2

### Army of Surprises – Surprised to hear the Army

September 28, 2004. We've backtracked a few years. I was still living with Mum then, since it all went pear-shaped down in Croydon. I must have been (let me think) twenty-three. The voices were still with me but I managed to deal with them pretty well.

Roughly four years had passed, which was a long time to get used to them. There would be certain occasions when it would even be possible to use them to my advantage, but generally – they were more of a hindrance than anything.

It would have been nice to be able to turn them on and off with a switch, but it didn't work like that. I definitely had my bad days, but then again – so does everyone. My bad days were just a little different.

One thing I was still adamant about was that the voices were real. There was no schizophrenia: the chemicals in my brain were fine. Medication would just turn me into a zombie if I took it properly. The few times I'd been back to see the psychiatrist were about as helpful as a car with no wheels. The answers I'd get off him were fresh out of a textbook, yet it had to be done to keep Mum happy. As far as she was concerned – I had this illness; I was dealing with it the best I could and was taking the medication. If that was enough to prevent her from worrying, then it was definitely worth it.

The voices were real (I'd made a mental note), and there was a reason why I could hear them – I just didn't know what it was.

Now I've already said people have bad days. Well, at the time, I wasn't too sure if September 28, 2004 was a bad day or not for me, yet it's definitely a significant day, and one worth talking about.

I'll skip to about three o'clock in the afternoon. It was a Tuesday. I was at my Mum's house, sitting at the kitchen table, painting one of my pictures. It was pouring down outside, and no one was home. My latest creation was starting to look like a big blue face with a huge gob.

"Gobsmacked! That's what I'll call this one," I said to myself. "I like that, yeah."

I took a big swig of coffee as if to celebrate. It must have been my sixth cup of coffee of the day and I was starting to vibrate. I really was vibrating – seriously! No wait – it was my phone. I pulled it from my pocket to see who was calling but I'd been concentrating so hard on my picture, that the screen was a blur.

I answered, with curiosity: "Hello?"

"All right bruv, Marcus here, how's it going?"

"Oh, hello mate," I replied in a relieved tone. "How are you?"

It was always a nice surprise to hear from Marcus, especially now he had this new girlfriend called Lotty, who took up so much of his time. No one really liked Lotty. She was a bit … Well she was fine to be fair. She made my brother happy, and that's what mattered (silly moo).

"I'm surviving – just about, you know," he said. "What you up to, Mr William?"

"Just finishing a picture round at Mum's. To be honest I'm a bit bored mate, what you doing?" I asked.

"Not a lot, bruv. Got a day off today, but Lotty's doing my nut right in at the moment."

"Oh yeah, I see." (How many times had I heard that one?)

"Yeah she is,bruv. I was just phoning to see if you fancied meeting up for a beer?" he asked, and judging by the tone of his voice – I figured he could use one.

"Love to, mate," I answered. "Shall we say – hmmm, Dibdabs? In, let's see – an hour?"

"Spot on, bruv, see you then," he said, followed by, "There's something I want to tell you anyway."

"Oh yeah, what's that then?" I asked inquisitively.

"Ah, tell you when I see you. See you soon."

I put the phone down and started to tidy up. That's the problem with pastels – they make such a flaming mess.

Now Dibdabs was our favourite bar in town. Clueless as to why exactly – there was never anyone in there, the beer was pretty poor, and the music was rubbish. They did have this soft, black leather sofa though. It was so comfortable, and because no one drank there – we always got it.

I looked out of the kitchen window, the rain was still beating down heavily.

'Better get a bus Will, and put your coat on, don't you think?' I said.

I did that a lot. No, not get on buses and put coats on! I mean talk to myself. It was one of the ways of dealing with things since my, (what shall we call it?), 'accident'.

After rushing around trying to locate my coat, I grabbed my keys, vacated the house, and entered the downpour. It was torrential! It being three-forty, the bus was due any minute, so I raced to the bus stop.

The Number Eight arrived a few minutes late, which was surprisingly good for round here. I jumped straight on, paid my ninety pence, and sat down towards the front.

There were no other passengers on the bus, just myself – clearly the only person stupid enough to be out in such weather.

The rain bombarded the bus windows with such force, that it made it difficult to see anything going on outside.

"Lovely day boss, isn't it?" The driver pointed out.

"Terrific," I replied; "bit wet though, don't you think?" I added.

"Yeah you could say that boss, could say that."

I smiled, sat back and relaxed in my chair, my eyes fixed to the huge droplets of water, crashing next to my head.

Unfortunately, my tranquil state of mind was soon disturbed, as the sound of all that water banging against the windows began to call up unfamiliar voices. There were lots of them too. The sheer volume of raindrops meant that I was able to hear a whole crowd of people on this bus.

A quick look round reinforced the fact that I was actually travelling alone, and a glance at the driver through his rear view mirror, proved that he wasn't making a peep. It had to be those voices – had to be: my own personal whatevers, once again making me unnecessarily paranoid, as I sat on the Number Eight.

Five minutes previous, I was a happy little bunny, and then as sudden as a heart attack, I'd been skinned in my seat, dangled upside down by my legs, ready to be dropped into a big pot of boiling water. And all because it was raining. Sometimes that's all it takes. Best solution is to snap out of it – pronto! Unfortunately this is easier said than done. Once a seed has been planted by those elusive gits, they leave you on a very slippery slope indeed.

I didn't need this now. I needed to be on the ball to meet Marcus – not a bundle of useless nerves. At my worst – it would have been just as productive to meet up with a Chinese speaking goat, rather than my brother. The point of no return was approaching quickly as I sat there shaking. I needed a distraction – fast!

And then it happened: as we crossed over the Severn and into town, there was a girl outside pushing a blue pushchair along the pavement, half-walking, half-jogging. It was difficult to see clearly, but she appeared to be wearing all black clothes and boots, with dark, shoulder length hair. Whoever was in that pushchair was certainly safe from the elements, yet the girl pushing looked soaked to the skin.

The bus drove past as I watched the girl until she was out of sight. I felt sorry she must have been so wet, but glad that the child was nice and snug under that plastic rain cover. It was a strange feeling: she never looked at the bus, and I did not recognise her, but for some reason – she stuck in my mind. In fact she stuck in my mind so much, that there was no longer any space left for the voices. Just as suddenly as the close shave with the hot pot, my fur had grown back and I'd returned to being the same happy bunny that had left the house, barely half an hour before.

As the bus reached the traffic lights next to the station, I stood up and looked around to make sure I hadn't left anything behind – bit silly really considering I didn't have anything in the first place. It was just then, that I noticed a white carrier-bag on one of the seats towards the back.

As I focused on the solitary bag, my initial thought was that it could be a bomb of some description, and to steer well clear. The right thing to do was to alert the driver and go about my day. Be that as it may, my curiosity got the better of me. As the bus sat fixed on red, I found myself approaching the suspect package.

A quick examination revealed that there were no explosives after all; just an expensive looking designer coat, and a small, suede-like box containing a gold ring. I could only assume the ring belonged to a woman, due to how dainty it was. Any man would do well to have fitted it on even his little finger.

Whoever did own the bag was certainly not on the bus, so I decided to pick it up and give it to the driver. As we pulled into stand-B, he informed me that the best thing to do would be to hand it into 'lost-property', situated inside the station's information kiosk.

The bus doors opened and I jumped off; thanked the driver and located the kiosk. I approached the counter with the bag and plonked it on the desk. The lady behind the counter took the bag off me and checked its contents. I explained to her the situation and so she then jotted down my details and enlightened me with the fact, that if no one claimed the package within twelve months – I could keep it for myself.

Not a bad deal for such a small deed, and I knew that someone would probably be missing their possessions, so on leaving the kiosk I felt happy – like I'd done something positive with my day (it's surprisingly nice to be nice you know).

It was still pelting down outside, so I scurried through the adjoining shopping centre to avoid getting unnecessarily wet. I couldn't wait to see Marcus as I rushed down the escalator, through the automatic doors, and onto the high street. *Dibdabs* was located a few hundred yards down the road. The anticipation of seeing Marcus, along with the natural urge to escape such horrendous weather conditions, saw me there in record time.

I walked through the swinging doors and into the bar. Boy it was a relief to be out of that rain. I took off my coat and looked at the green neon clock behind the bar, only to realise that in my urgency, I'd arrived fifteen minutes early. The pub was completely desolate (no surprise there), except for Dave the barman wearing his usual long, black leather jacket. We all called him 'Matrix Dave' because he always walked round clutching his mobile phone, as if he was looking for an exit.

He was slumped over the corner of the bar, reading a daily tabloid, with a look of eternal misery plastered all over his morbid, greasy yellow face. I walked over as he straightened himself out and quickly turned over the page he'd been engrossed in – I'll give you (page) three guesses which one. I smirked to myself as I approached. I was probably the first sign of life he'd seen all day.

"Blimey, it's a lovely day out there, isn't it," stated Dave. Sarcasm didn't suit him though.

"Yeah you're right: busy in here isn't it?" I replied. "Everybody's wandering about outside, looking for an entrance," I added.

Dave wasn't my favourite barman in the world: just another reason why I didn't have a clue why I drank there. That sofa was so bloody comfortable though. I paid for two beers and proceeded towards the shiny leather couch. It was right at the back of the pub next to the fireman.

Now I know that sounds a bit weird, but the owner collected statues, which were displayed all around his establishment. He had a fireman, Elvis, James Dean, plus an angry Orc, to name but a few. The police officer next to the front door was probably another reason why no one drank there.

I raised my pint to my mouth, when suddenly the door swung open.

Marcus entered.

"All right bruv?" he bellowed out across the whole length of the pub, and then: "All right Daaaaave? Busy in here isn't it?" he quipped, as he walked past the bar and over to our table. He whipped off his raincoat and folded it over the back of one of the stools. I slid over to one side to accommodate Marcus' skinny little beanbag. After all, this sofa was probably the only thing he liked here too.

He plonked himself down next to me and grabbed his beer. Before he said another word to me, he'd guzzled half of his pint and sat back.

"Ahhh: needed that bruv I'm telling you," he said.

He seemed agitated, and within a minute he'd pulled out his phone and was playing with the buttons. I just sat there and observed him intently, as he acted in this peculiar fashion.

"Is everything okay, Marcus?" I asked, but my question didn't seem to register, as he continued to push buttons as if his life depended on it. He took another big swig of his drink as I asked him again: "Everything okay mate?"

"What? Oh – yeah – sorry bruv, everything's fine. It's just Lotty – she's doing my head in a bit." His eyes still fixated on his phone.

"Why, what's up mate?" I questioned.

"Oh it doesn't matter – I'll tell you later."

He knocked back the rest of his drink and slid his empty glass across the table. He then stood up hastily as I watched in amazement at his actions.

"Another beer?" he asked, as he reached deep into his front pocket and jingled his loose change with his hand.

"I've barely started this one yet mate," I said, raising my 'almost full' glass as a means of demonstrating how desperate he was to down his pints.

"Well drink up then," he ordered. He gave me one of his cheeky smiles and headed for the bar.

"What's wrong with him then?" I asked the fireman. "He's never this tense – especially his day off. Don't worry, I'll find out what the problem is."

I took a large swig of my beer, licked the froth from my lips, and waited for Marcus to return. Marcus is younger than I am. Let's see – he would have been nineteen at the time. We used to play-fight a lot when he was still a kid. I used to pick him up and throw him all over the shop, but since moving back from Croydon, he'd outgrown me, and I was a bit more dubious about starting anything. Not quite the irritating, flimsy little brat I'd remembered.

He used to be so naughty. I remember this one time; he got hold of Mum's sewing kit and stuck a load of pins in my mattress. I nearly woke the whole street up when I got into bed that night: my hip hadn't felt quite the same since! Still, it was nice to be able to go out and have a few beers with the lad.

Anyway, we had been in *Dibdabs* for a few hours now: it was starting to get a bit dark outside and the rain was still coming down hard. The neon clock behind the bar read 6:10. Marcus and I were on our fourth beer, sitting on the same sofa, just discussing random topics when suddenly – the pub door swung open. We halted our conversation and switched our attention to the entrance. After all – this was the first time the thing had opened since we got there!

Stepping onto the grimy wooden floorboards was this girl. She was dressed in a black cardigan, together with black trousers and dark, high-heeled boots on. She was drenched through. We watched as she promenaded across the pub, her heels tapping on the wood with every stride. Her top was dripping everywhere, as she hoisted herself up onto one of the high-stools at the bar.

I could see Dave's eyes light up as she reached for her purse. This must have been the highlight of his day – by far. I'm not sure what drink she ordered, but it came in a tall glass with a straw.

"Anyway bruv, I hope you've remembered your Mum's birthday next week," said Marcus.

There was a muted pause as I continued to gape at the girl. She looked just like the girl I'd seen with the pushchair earlier, on the way into town. There was no pushchair with her this time, but I was convinced it was she. I could see her more clearly too. Under the pink neon strip running along the glass-shelf I could see her face. She was an angel – an absolute angel: a pissed-off angel by the looks of it, judging by her homicidal expression, and she was sure sucking the life out of that drink!

"Will – Will – wake up mate – Will," Marcus repeated, clicking his fingers in front of my mesmerised face.

"Uh, yea-yeah mate," I spluttered.

"Your Mum's birthday next week – have you remembered?"

I turned and looked at him, trying my hardest to register what was being asked of me, when suddenly it clicked: "Oh sugar, Mum's birthday!" I gasped. "No I completely forgot. That's okay though, I'll get something sorted. In fact I'm working on a new painting she might like – it's called 'Gobsmacked'."

"Flaming hell bruv: you give her one of your crazy pictures – she will be gobsmacked!" exclaimed Marcus. "Anyway, I'm getting bored with this place – let's get out of here."

I concluded he was right, so we finished our beers, coated up, and headed for the exit.

Now, at this point I'm not sure what was running through my mind, nor did I have any idea of what I would achieve, but something inside told me I couldn't leave without saying something to the girl sitting at the bar. Usually my confidence is pretty low when it comes to chatting up the ladies but for some reason (probably four pints), I found myself tugging on Marcus' sleeve and signalling him to wait a second.

He stood by the door next to the police officer and watched, bewildered, as I approached the girl. I had my arms pointed out either side of me, wobbling along like some sort of intoxicated penguin. She was facing away from me as I stepped closer and closer. She must have caught a reflection of me homing in, through the mirror under the optics, and before I could say anything, she swung round on her stool to face me, stopping me in my tracks. I froze, and pulled a stupid face, as if I'd been caught stealing penny sweets from the corner shop.

"What do you want?" she said rudely, or was I being rude approaching her in the first place? My new-found confidence was instantly shattered as I struggled to think of something to say, while still pulling the same stupid face.

"Don't suppose that was you walking near the bridge earlier, with your pushchair, was it?" I mustered. "You just looked familiar, that's all." (What a plum!)

"What's it to you, yafreakoid?" she answered.

I could see Marcus out of the corner of my eye, hiding his face under his over-sized collar, probably loving every second of my embarrassing situation. Even Dave was smirking, as he gawked at his newspaper that he probably wasn't even reading. I felt like landing him one. As a matter of fact, it would have been nice to have grabbed him by that stupid leather matrix jacket, and shoved a selection of blue and red pills down his stupid throat, to finally launch him through a permanent exit into oblivion. He could take his precious mobile phone with him, the phone that half his wages must have been spent on, so he could receive pictures of hot girls in his area. I pulled my screw-face at him instead. Violence was not going to help me successfully clinch myself a date with this sweetie. I tried to continue my little rhapsody: "So then, I don't suppose a little dazzler like you would feel inclined to . . .?" I was quickly interrupted.

"Listen, you stupid little toss-pot, I'm not in the mood for this. I'm having a really bad day. I've got a splitting headache. So why don't you, and your friend, just leave me alone, okay?"

It was time to go – immediately. I turned around and headed for the door. Marcus held the door open for me, struggling to hold back his tears.

As soon as we got outside, he couldn't help himself. He blurted out in uncontrollable laughter at my dismay. It was his signature laugh and he only used it when something was really funny. His laugh was so funny that it made me laugh, and soon we were both a dribbling mess, keeled over on the pavement being soaked from above.

"Where to next then, smooth boy?" he joked.

I had to admit, the previous beverages plus the failed attempt at liaison had put me in the mood for an extended night of boozing.

Marcus informed me that his mum and step-dad were staying on a caravan park in Wales for the week, so he had a free house. He lived with his mum on the other side of town. The idea of a free house sounded perfect, especially considering that I still lived with my mum. Still – better phone her, and let her know what I'm doing. After all – she does worry.

That night we toured the pubs till we could hardly walk, let alone talk. By half-twelve we were steaming. The rain had stopped so we decided that walking home was probably the most stupid, but best, idea. This wasn't before Marcus decided to stumble into the local pizza joint, and order a fifteen-inch spicy special with chilli sauce and extra jalapenos.

Now I'm not going to lie to you – this pizza was hot! In fact, for the next few days I was frightened of passing wind. After walking and falling all the way to Marcus' (which took nearly an hour), I'd nearly finished a whole slice. That would be my only slice – my mouth was so hot, you could probably light a cigarette on my tongue. How Marcus managed to scoff the other fourteen-and-a-half inches I do not know. Knowing him, he was probably in agony, but he liked to show off.

After messing about at the front door of his mum's trying to get the key in the hole, we staggered into the hall. The next challenge was to find the light-switch without breaking anything. I tried to stand still and wait for visibility before attempting to move (this was harder than it sounds).

After that little obstacle, Marcus led me into the front room, directed me to the leather couch, and turned the TV on. He then went through to the kitchen, whilst I clumsily tried to operate the remote, and select a music channel. From what I could work out, they were all rubbish.

Soon, Marcus barged through the sitting-room door, carrying a box of his step-dad's beers, with a huge grin on his face. He fell next to me, pulled out a couple of tins and cracked one open. Sitting on that sofa, with the crap music on the box, I felt like I was back in *Dibdabs* again. I too cracked opened my beer, had a swig and lounged back. We didn't say much as we lay there, trying to hold our drinks without spilling any. We just listened to the music and gazed at the ceiling.

The room was spinning! I tried to focus on various objects around the room, which was also a struggle by this time. On the sideboard I did notice a small photograph in a shiny gold frame. As I tried to focus on the picture, I noticed that it was a man in some kind of uniform. In questioning Marcus as to who it was, he informed me that it was his brother Alistair – his older brother from his mum's side.

"Ah, Ali," I said. "He's in the army, isn't he?" I queried.

"That's right bruv. Ali – Ali the don."

He pulled himself from his seat, wobbled over to the sideboard and returned with the photo.

I'd met Alistair a long time ago when he was on leave, but didn't really know him. Marcus never really spoke of him much, but I did know that he adored him.

"That photo was taken the day he 'passed out' for the army," Marcus told me. "Look at how proud he is!"

I had to admit, he did look like a proud man: suit all perfect, with gleaming boots on the end of his razor-sharp trousers.

"Fair play to him," I said, but by now it was starting to become increasingly more difficult to stay awake.

"Yeah, fair play to him – you're right Will," he replied. "He's a sergeant now, bruv, a sergeant. He looks a lot different than that now though: a proper don."

I smiled at Marcus as he looked at the photo – clearly deep in thought.

"Actually bruv, that's what I wanted to talk to you about," he said, slurring but trying to sound serious.

I put my can down on the carpet and curled up against the armrest.

"What's that mate?" I sighed.

"Well the thing is bruv," he continued.

"Is?" My eyes started to shut uncontrollably.

"I'm joining the army."

"That's nice Marcus, good for you mate," I said, but not really taking anything in. I was on a one-way shuttle to noddy land and nothing could stop me.

I yawned, and soon – I was asleep.

"Goodnight bruv," sighed Marcus, as he stretched his arms above his head, and he too – drifted off.

Morning came for me at about nine-thirty. A constant thudding sound coming from outside awoke me. Boy did my head hurt: I didn't need this irritating noise too. I opened the long draping curtains out onto the back garden to see the neighbours laying what looked to be a patio. I wished they would just shut up – my head was pounding. I looked at Marcus who was still dormant on the couch. How he could sleep through all that racket I do not know. He was snoring his head off – dead to the world, covered in chilli sauce.

I just sat back down on the sofa not wishing to disturb him. The terrible music was still playing from the night before, which was subsequently replaced with a breakfast programme.

Uh, breakfast – no thanks! That slice of pizza had unsettled my stomach. The pizza I could remember, I mean – how could I forget something that dangerous? But pretty much everything else was a bit fuzzy.

I knew it had been raining: the bottoms of my jeans were still wet and the garden looked sodden. It was a nice morning – fresh yet sunny. My beer can was sat down on the floor, hardly touched.

Right next to the sofa was what appeared to be a photo-frame facing the magnolia carpet. I reached down and picked it up. It was a photo of Marcus' brother Ali. He was dressed in his army uniform. I seemed to recall thinking that it was a photo of when he 'passed out'. He looked quite young in the photo, although I knew he was older than I was now.

I was just about to put the photo out of harm's way when suddenly it clicked. We'd had a conversation about him last night.

"That's right, of course." It came back to me: "He's a sergeant now."

I stood up and placed the photo on top of the television – that's where it looked like it belonged.

Marcus remained asleep on the sofa, sounding like some sort of caged prehistoric animal. I quietly tiptoed past him and went upstairs to use the bathroom. Whilst washing my hands, I recalled Marcus cracking a joke about joining the army himself.

"Ha, that was a good one mate," I chuckled.

Marcus had spent the last three years working for his uncle's air-conditioning company and things were looking pretty good. He had days off more or less when he wanted, a good wage and an uncle (who cherished him) for a boss – lovely. There was no way on this planet he was joining the army – why would he?

Anyway, I came back downstairs to find him perked up, and awake. The chain on the toilet must have woken him: mind you, those noisy neighbours were still at it.

"Bloody hell, Marcus, you look worse than I feel," I jested.

"Cheers bruv," he replied. "You look pretty awful yourself. Hey – bloody good night though, don't you think?"

"Yeah think so," I said. "Can't really remember much, to be honest."

"Oh, I can bruv, I remember everything."

He looked at me with a smug look on his face. He had me worried now, so I told him to fill in the blanks.

"*Dibdabs*? Remember being in there?" he said.

"Yeah, vaguely. Why, what about it?" I wondered.

"On the way out? Ring any bells does it?" he continued.

"Sorry mate, you've completely lost me," I said calmly, yet panicking within.

"The girl in black sitting at the bar? Yes? No?"

Suddenly the penny dropped. My face turned from a look of confusion, to one of stunned realisation.

"Remember now? Captain Smooooooth," he giggled, as my mouth opened wider than it was supposed to go.

I sat down.

"Oh balls! I remember now," and I did. I remembered what I'd said, what she said to me, and even what she looked like. She was beautiful – I definitely remembered that.

"You plonker," said Marcus.

"I know, what an idiot," I admitted, but still, there was something about that girl I liked – just not sure what. She was an angel though – definitely an angel.

Suddenly Marcus changed the subject.

"Hey what's that picture of Ali doing on top of the TV?"

"Oh sorry mate. It was on the floor, I just put it there."

"No bruv, Ali doesn't live on top of the TV: he lives over here."

He picked up the photo, put it back on the sideboard, and adjusted it; as if there was a perfect position for it to be.

"There that's better: sorry Ali," he said to the photo whilst patting it with the palm of his hand.

I looked at him thinking 'what a weird boy!' But then I thought about all the strange things that I did sometimes, so I suppose it wasn't that odd.

"Anyway, what do you think about it, bruv?" asked Marcus.

"Think about what?" I said.

"You know: what I told you about last night."

"And what was that then, mate?" I queried.

"About me joining the army, you idiot," he told me.

I looked at him with a frown.

"Yeah, but you were only joking though – right?"

No he wasn't joking. He sat down next to me and told me how he'd already passed his medical and other tests. He even had a start date for basic training – March 14, 2005.

"Bloody hell, Marcus," I said. "I don't know what to say – congratulations I suppose – you nutter."

Talk about surprises.

I dishevelled his hair with my fingers, and smiled, and yet inside I felt gutted.

Like my picture – gobsmacked!

## CHAPTER 3

## The Problem with Balloon Rides

For those of you who are unfamiliar with Shrewsbury, there's an old market hall at the town's centre. There's a tall clock tower, with white hands and a large spike on top, that's just crying out to get struck by lightning. The market's right underneath – you can't miss it (it's probably the most grotesque building ever to be constructed in the town's history).

Inside you can find a whole range of quality, local, produce, such as fruit 'n' veg, meat and cheese, to name but a few.

Upstairs on the gallery there's a second hand bookstall. I know this because it's my Dad's (that's Gordon to you).

Now Dad loves books – loves them. I mean he sees a 'first edition' like a 'beautiful woman' – he's that obsessed!

He opened the stall a while back now, since his partner Susan refused to store his out-of-control collection in the house any longer. They were protruding from the drawers, cupboards, the wardrobe; he even had a stack of them in the downstairs lavatory.

So – solution: open a bookstall. Then he could spend all day with his precious books if he wanted to (which he did), so that's what happened.

And what would his new stall be named? I'll tell you - *Books*, that's what. It was perfect. Everybody knew what he sold – it was obvious.

Trouble was, his new-found space soon became just as cluttered as the house, so before you knew it the stall next door was his. So what would he call this stall? I'll tell you that too – *More Books*. It was genius, for now everyone knew there were more books for sale.

*Even More Books* was his third venture and by now the pennies were really rolling in; so after he got his hands on a fourth stall – it was time for a piece of the action myself. I mean, he had half the gallery! It was daunting.

I'd decided to sell second-hand videos in this unit (which was yet to be named). I would patrol the charity shops – all twenty-something that Shrewsbury has to offer, as well as car-boot sales and fairs; a lot like Dad. It was the perfect combination.

The day was February 7, 2005. Dad had just celebrated his sixtieth birthday the previous week, and had been given a ticket for a hot air balloon ride from Susan. He'd always wanted to go on a balloon ride, but the trouble was that the ticket was for the following Saturday – National Book Day. Unfortunately, the ticket was non-transferable and yet there was no way that Dad was going to miss out on the weekend trade.

Now usually in a situation like this, he'd give his pal Richard a tinkle to come in and cover. Unfortunately for dad, Richard was on a walking expedition that weekend, so that was the end of that.

He'd never asked me before but, on the Monday in question, I received the call. The market didn't open on a Monday so Dad was home, studying maps of the countryside ready for his big day. He must have been trying to solve the problem about the market and, after ringing around, concluded that I was his final hope.

So out came the question, to which I replied:

"Yeah, course I can Dad, no problem," surprised but happy he'd asked. "On one condition though."

"Oh yes, and what's that then?" he muttered. (He should have guessed there'd be a catch).

"I'm allowed to take my portable television with me, okay?"

Unlike Dad, I'm not much of a book lover. In fact, I've never read a book off my own back – well – ever. With TV it's right there in front of you: there's no need to concentrate, and for me, concentration was never one of my virtues.

"Okay then – deal," he agreed. "I'll drop the keys off at your mum's after work on Friday. Oh, and don't screw this up!"

Mum would have been fine with Dad popping round. They got divorced when I was still a kid, but always remained (sort of) friends. They were both happy now, which wouldn't have been the case if they had stayed together, so there was no problem.

I was excited about the proposal, and sure enough – Saturday came. That morning I was up at half-five. I hadn't been up that early for years: not since the Croydon days when I'd do the breakfast shift.

I wasn't used to being awake at such a time and needed two coffees in a row just to function properly. The market doors opened at seven, but I wanted to be there slightly early to get my bearings.

Mum at the time, lived just a ten-minute walk away from the market. It was a crisp morning, yet as I left the house and looked up, there was not a cloud in sight. Everything seemed still except for the occasional car driving by as I headed into town. There was hardly any wind either and I remember thinking what a great day it was to go ballooning.

The market hall was in my sight. Now, at this point, it was actually the voices in my head which suddenly made me realise that I'd forgotten to bring my bloody television.

This was all I needed as I stood by the road, pondering what to do. How was I supposed to carry the damned thing anyway? It was half-six, and after standing there for a minute or so, I decided to walk back to Mum's and book a taxi. There was no way on God's green earth I'd be going to work without my telly – no way, so I turned round and briskly headed back.

I remember Dad telling me not to screw up that day. You could say arriving twenty-five minutes late wasn't too bad for me. Still, there was hardly anyone around as I walked through the doors, just the flower lady and a handful of traders setting up their stalls. Most of them had probably been doing this for most of their working lives.

I felt a bit silly: walking through carrying a sodding television in my arms. But everyone just seemed oblivious to everything, unless it had something to do with what they were doing.

I climbed the four flights of concrete steps onto the gallery, weighed down by my TV. It wasn't till reaching the top I remembered that there was a lift. Clearly I still wasn't functioning properly so decided (considering there were no patrons about) to grab another coffee from the caff – also on the gallery.

It came in one of those polystyrene cups: the kind that you can't help but chew around the rim. I grabbed a pew on one of the bright orange, moulded seats and knocked back my caffeine hit. I picked up my TV and headed out of the café when suddenly I heard:

"Hey. You just going to leave that there are you?" I turned around to see a tea lady (of which there were three) pointing towards my empty cup.

"Oh sorry," I said, put my TV back down, and grabbed the cup off the table. The lady's finger then changed direction and aimed towards the bin. I thought 'you lazy git, there's three of you,' but still I discarded my cup and left. After turning up late the last thing I wanted to do was have a run-in with the tea lady. After all, Dad must have been a regular, so I just smiled on my way out – clearly not used to market etiquette yet.

On reaching Dad's stall, I put the telly down and spent a minute or two just standing on the balcony, watching the traders below as they rushed around in their own little worlds. It was funny to think that all of this was happening every day (except Sundays and Mondays) whilst I was still tucked up in my warm bed. At the same time there was a nice feeling about it all.

Next, I pulled the keys from my pocket (at least I hadn't forgotten to bring them) and started to open the rusty iron shutters protecting Dad's pride and joy. As I unlocked the fourth unit, I looked up to see that Dad had finally named this one too. *Books and Videos* it read in large black capitals. I chuckled, thinking 'clever dad,' and raised the squeaky barrier.

"I think I'll set up the TV in this stall," I decided.

I felt more at home surrounded by my videos: at least I knew a bit about videos. And then it struck me. What the hell was going to happen when someone asks me about books and I haven't got the foggiest idea what they're talking about?

"Oh don't worry Will. Just cross that bridge when you come to it," I accepted.

I made a table for my TV out of a couple of cardboard boxes and plugged in. It was one of those new integrated digital jobs, with the thousand extra useless channels. Mum had bought it me for Christmas – it must have cost a bomb.

I think everyone made a special effort last year. Marcus was round at ours for Christmas day. It was to be the last Christmas we'd spend with him before he went into the army. I don't think any of us were looking forward to that.

Even though it was only basic training, nobody was under any illusion (including Marcus), that one day – considering the world's current state of affairs – he'd be sent to war.

Still, didn't have to worry about that for now – I'd got a bookstall to run.

Before doing anything else though I turned on the TV, only to find a fuzzy screen. I checked the aerial – everything fine; flicked through the multiple channels desperate to see a picture – still nothing. After about ten minutes of hopelessly pushing buttons and whacking the top of the TV, I finally got a signal. A bloke wearing a suit, sitting behind a news desk had saved me. Unfortunately, it was the twenty-four hour news channel, so I guessed I'd probably be seeing a lot of him considering I was too scared to fiddle about anymore.

I sat back in Dad's favourite deckchair, and waited for some action.

By nine o'clock there were quite a few shoppers in the market, and by ten I was really getting into the swing of things. In fact, there wasn't really any time to watch TV. Even when it was quiet I found myself browsing through bookshelves, in the hope of being a bit more helpful to the next customer than the last.

Some of Dad's regulars came in, wondering who this strange young man was running the stall. Most were just bookworms though: simply there to buy something because they thought they had to (being National Book Day and all) and hopefully go home with a bargain. Luckily, Dad's stock was already priced up, so that part was easy.

Now and again I'd sell a few videos, which put me on a real high.

Crazy visions of having my own stall entered my head, a stall where I could sell my pictures too.

"Yeah, you could do that Will," I said. "You could even paint them here." Then I thought of how hard it was getting up that morning, which did put me off the idea.

Shortly after contemplating this, the record stall on the other side of the gallery was just opening – it was almost eleven o'clock.

'Yeah, you've got the right idea mate,' I thought. I mean – who's going to be up at seven o'clock to buy some vinyl? Most of his customers would probably just be going to bed at that time.

The stall was called '*Market Spinners*' and was the only other stall on the gallery: the only other stall due to the fact that Dad had most of them, and the ones that did try setting up there always failed. This was mainly due to the fact they always sold crap no one wanted.

I mean, who in their right mind would walk into a market and buy a foot spa for fifty quid. Who would really want to receive an Indian head massage right next to a record stall pumping out rave music, whilst you've got Joe the fruit 'n' veg man underneath, selling avocados 'two for a pound'. It was enough to give you an Indian headache more than anything.

There was a bit of a lull around lunchtime, yet the cash bag strapped to my waist already felt quite heavy. I was thinking that Dad would be proud. I pictured him, up in that hot air balloon taking in the magnificent views, and, at the same time, panicking like mad about his dear son running things back on earth.

Susan was afraid of heights, so she had decided to race around the countryside in her sports car. Her plan was to try and keep up with the balloon and meet Dad when he landed. That's the problem with hot air balloons – how do you know where they're going to land? Undoubtedly the wind just takes them whichever way it's blowing – doesn't it? You can't control that surely. They must have a licence to land wherever the hell they can or something. 'I'm sure Dad will fill me in when he gets back,' I thought.

Whilst there were no customers to serve, I thought it would be a good time to eat. I'd forgotten that the cheese and onion sandwich I'd made the night before was still in my coat pocket. It must have got a bit squashed in the process of transporting the television, as it no longer resembled much of a sandwich. Still, I removed it from its wrapping and tucked in.

I was in the fourth unit (*Books and Videos*) devouring my excuse for a sandwich, as I arranged my videos back to their former order. I wasn't really paying much attention to the news on the TV, but catching a glimpse I noticed a news flash – something about a building of some description collapsing – a block of flats maybe – I wasn't really sure. The aerial footage showed scenes of fire engines and ambulances surrounding a big mound of smoking rubble. It looked like chaos.

However my attention was soon distracted when a man popped his head round the corner asking for assistance in the next unit. I plonked my sarnie down on top of the TV and went to serve him.

Now, if I had known who my next customer was to be I'd have probably shut the shop there and then and bolted out through the fire exit. As it happened – I was too late. I was watching the people below from the balcony, just eating the remains of my sandwich when suddenly, at the end of the landing – the elevator doors opened. I watched in horror. The wheels of a blue pushchair emerged from the lift, followed by a girl in a denim skirt with a black cardigan. Her hair was cut short but there was no doubt it was she – the girl at *Dibdabs* from months ago – the one I'd completely humiliated myself in front of. I'd pretty much forgotten about that little incident but now she was back – back to haunt me.

Scenarios flooded through my head, I dithered in a state of panic as she stepped onto the gallery. Maybe she was just using the toilet (also upstairs), or maybe she was just getting a cup of tea from the café. Perhaps it was her boyfriend who ran the record stall, even. No – she was headed straight towards me.

My heart raced as she advanced closer and closer. All I wanted to do was get the hell out of there, but that just wasn't an option.

"I know, Will. Just hide behind a bookshelf till she goes away," I decided.

Now I know I told you earlier about some of my good ideas – this wasn't one of them. I sneaked into the third unit (*Even More Books*) and squeezed myself between one of the cabinets and the brick wall. I stood there, silently hoping she would go away. The sound of hardbacks being shuffled about in the next unit, along with the noise only an infant could make, confirmed my fears that it was she. I prayed to mighty God she'd just disappear soon, whilst I stood, cramped up tight against the wall like some sort of moron.

"Please just go away," I whispered, "please."

It felt like an eternity being squashed behind there, impersonating my cheese sandwich, when suddenly – my nightmare became true.

In between a gap in the books I saw her wheel the pushchair around the corner with a book under her arm, looking for assistance. I trembled. A book fell off the cabinet onto the hard floor in front of her with a great thud. I'd been exposed. No choice now but to climb out and assist.

"Don't worry, Will, it's okay," I tried to convince myself. "Just play it cool son – nice and cool."

I struggled to free myself from my self-created hole, covered in cobwebs and other various accumulated debris. The girl just watched in confusion as I brushed myself down while at the same time, tried to look as if there was a good reason for me to be behind there. The little boy in the pushchair looked equally bemused, as I humiliated myself in front of his mother for a second time.

"Hi there Madam, how can I help you?" I said, with a painfully false smile across my face, in the vain hope she wouldn't recognise me.

"Oh dear: it's you," she replied, destroying instantly any hopes I had. "What on earth are you doing behind there?"

"Think quick, Will – think quick."

"Umm – oh, a book fell off the top and I was just getting it," I claimed.

The girl nodded her head slowly, raising her eyebrows as if to acknowledge my fib. I tried to cover the lie by quickly focusing my attention on the boy.

"Hello young man, so what's your name then?" I said to him, crouching down in front of his chair; but, in return, he just looked at me in the same baffled manner as his mother.

"That's my son, Matty. He doesn't really talk much – especially to plonkers," she said.

"Oh that's terrific," I replied. "How old is he?"

"He's one-and-a-bit," she answered. "So what's your name you weird, weird boy?"

"I'm Will and before you go any further, I'd just like to apologise for being such a plank when I saw you in *Dibdabs* that day."

"Oh don't worry about it, Will. I'm sorry too," she said. "It's just that I was having an incredibly bad day and you caught me at the wrong time that's all. In fact, you made me laugh, I thought it was funny. Didn't really mean you were a freak though, but now I'm not so sure."

"Oh no a book really did fall behind there – honest," I said defensively.

"Yeah of course it did, so where is it?" she quizzed.

"Couldn't quite reach it but don't worry, I'll get it later," I answered, quickly followed by: "so anyway, which one is it you're interested in?"

With a big grin across her face, she passed me the book from under her arm. I looked at the cover to see that it was called *Fifty Years of Murder*.

"Crikey," I said, "what do you want a book like that for?"

"Need a few tips," she replied.

I looked at her, stunned, for a second and then said: "Why, you're not thinking about killing me are you?"

"Don't know yet," she answered. "It depends if you ask me any more stupid questions."

"Oh sorry: anyway that's umm . . ." I opened the front page to check the price. "That's four pounds, but to a gorgeous girl like yourself, you can have it for three."

"What! I can have it for free?" she joked.

"No – three. If you want it for free then you'll just have to murder me," I said.

"Don't tempt me Will, don't tempt me."

She opened her purse and handed me a note, which I put in the cash bag and pulled out her change.

She then told me she was thinking of doing a course in forensic medicine, and as the book was full of real-life cases, it could be of some interest. It was a relief, in a way, to realise she wasn't a complete psycho after all.

We talked (civilly) for a little while, as it was quiet. She also made me aware that the geezer downstairs, who Dad got his sausages off every week, was actually her step dad. I told her that this was my Dad's stall and I was just covering for the day. She wondered what Dad would think, if he knew that I jumped behind the bookshelves whenever a customer came (clearly not a stupid girl).

Anyway, after ten minutes or so of chat she said she was going. The air had been cleared and the ice was broken. This seemed to be a golden opportunity to redeem myself and ask her out – so I did.

"Hey listen, I know you think I'm a bit odd but I'm actually an okay bloke so if you wanted my number by any chance, if you're available at all and wanted to go out or something, or maybe just watch a film if you like films or not I don't know, then you can have my number – if you want that is."

I was thinking to myself that this attempt was almost as smooth as the first time I'd spoken to her, yet, against all the odds – she accepted, even though she did let me know that it was a pathetic effort.

She pulled out her phone and entered the digits whilst I stood there in disbelief.

"I'll call you," she promised.

She put her book under the kid's seat and left. I smiled and waved goodbye to little Matty as they headed for the elevator. I watched them walk down the landing; hoping she would turn around as some sort of assurance – but she never did. Still, I was delirious; smiling so hard that I nearly pulled a muscle! It felt great, and for the first time in a long time there was a spring in my step.

My good fortune seemed to have a knock-on effect with the bookstall too. The remainder of that afternoon was really busy, with some customers purchasing a few of Dad's rarer novels, making a great difference to the day's takings.

Just an hour to go and I still couldn't get the girl out of my head (after all – she was an angel). I was having a quick sort out when suddenly my face dropped. I stopped in my tracks, thinking what a cretin I was. In all the excitement I'd only forgotten to get her bloody name!

'Never mind Will, you can get it next time. She already thinks you're dense so this shouldn't be too much of a problem,' I concluded.

Four o'clock came and it was time to pack up. The stall was empty and the cash bag was full. The only thing left to do now was get my TV, which hadn't really received any attention all day. When I went to unplug it from the wall, the story on the news was still focusing on the collapsed building. It was obviously a major disaster but I was in too much of a hurry to take any notice. I wanted to get something to eat quickly, due to the fact that my previous sandwich hadn't really satisfied my hunger.

I checked and double-checked everything was in order, put my coat on, and closed the shutters. As I locked the last unit (*Books*), there was one book which grabbed my attention. It was a book on palmistry. There was a picture of a hand on the cover, with a map of all the hand's creases and their meanings.

Now I know I told you that I wasn't much of a book lover, yet this one seemed to have the potential to be an interesting read. It might even hold some sort of clue to why I was hearing these voices. Dad wouldn't mind if I borrowed it over the weekend, so I took it, along with my TV, which to be honest was getting on my nerves by this time.

The final shutter was locked and I was off. 'Good job, Will, you've excelled yourself today mate,' I thought to myself on the way down the stairs – oblivious to the lift, once again, in my state of pride.

That didn't matter though. I'd sold a load of books for Dad, as well as a handful of videos for myself which felt great. More importantly than this however, the girl of my dreams now had my number – even though her name was a mystery.

Stepping out onto the street, the wind had really picked up since the morning. I remember thinking that Dad would have been bloody miles away by now. I bet Susan was having difficulty keeping up – even in a sports car. I chuckled, and headed to the bus stop with my bulky, heavy telly.

'Hope you're having a good time, Dad. See you when you get back. Oh, and don't worry – everything's fine.'

## CHAPTER 4

## The Lines of Confusion

I know what it's like to be confused. It would be fair to say that I'm an expert in this field, considering that I suffer from disorientation so often. Bewilderment has become one of my regular states of mind.

It must run in the family or something because my Mum gets confused easily too. I'm not sure who's worse really. Mum gets confused over the remote control for the TV, so only the divine Lord himself would have an idea as to why she wanted Eric to buy her a laptop. It would probably take her the rest of her life to figure out how to turn the damned thing on! Still, she likes to think she's moving with the times, and she probably saw a laptop as a fashionable accessory; rather than a useful implement.

Eric's just as bad. He's okay if something's got an instruction manual, but if that new electric can opener didn't come with a step by step guide – then there'd be a problem. I'm not too bad with stuff like that: I'd say that I'm pretty up-to-speed on technology – although I don't really like a lot of it.

That night after working for Dad in the market, I was lying in bed watching the telly. Can't remember what programme I was watching but anyway, the commercials were on and I was thinking to myself that the world had gone mad.

These companies were advertising their new products; saying how revolutionary they are, and how we just can't live without them. I remember thinking 'what a load of rubbish.' How can these products possibly be revolutionary? How long exactly, can you continue to improve the same damned thing?

That's the way the world works these days. The television is (without a doubt) the most influential appliance ever to be invented, not to mention a vast means for advertisement. It's this rectangle piece of hardware that you plug into the wall, owned by almost every household, that's got us all hypnotised – day in, day out.

Now I'm not denying my own personal fondness for the television. I think they're great and if they were to suddenly disappear, I would probably miss them – but they cast no spells on me.

Let me put it this way. In a thousand years time (apart from being dead) I won't be rushing out to buy the new 'latest and greatest' vibrating razor, with fifteen blades that will rip your face off in one clean swoop.

You mark my words – I guarantee (assuming the world doesn't end) that by the twenty-fifth century, washing powder companies will still be bringing out two-in-one products that claim to get your clothes whiter and softer than ever before. Now that's got to be pretty white!

Cosmetics manufacturers will be bringing out their new mascara, which claims to create eyelashes that appear fifty percent longer than the previous year. Now if that carries on (and if there was any truth to it), then women (bless them) will end up walking the streets with great big broomsticks sticking out of their eyelids – it's a joke, and a very profitable one at that.

Advertising aside, the television is also influential enough to take a regular person, and either turn them into a god – or create a monster. People will listen too, because it's on the telly so it must be so. If it's not true, or didn't happen like it says it did, then why is it on the telly? The telly doesn't lie does it?

People have been able to use TV to get where they want to be in life. This is great, but on the flip side – people's lives (even innocent people) have been irreversibly destroyed. The nation's 'love to hate' nature is a dangerous fuel, which television feeds off greedily, with no real regard to the damage it can cause. At the end of the day, like advertising – it all boils down to money.

Yeah, I think television does have its advantages. We can gain a lot of knowledge by watching TV. We can learn about nature, food, and even space travel, for example. Kids can learn things from a young age, in a fun way. We can also keep up-to-speed with what's happening in the world by watching the news (not that this is always completely accurate).

Generally though, despite room for improvement – the benefits of TV are nice to have at the touch of a button, and now that everything has gone digital crazy – there's even more choice of what to watch.

However, the jump from five channels to umpteen of them, could potentially confuse a lot of us out there.

I think many people are confused, anyway. In fact, I reckon practically everyone is, and they don't even know it. People just seem to be able to block out their feelings and simplify everything without asking questions. They become robots of society who operate systematically, confined to a weekly routine that is programmed into their brain – so they don't even have to think about it.

Monday – do the shopping: Tuesday – put the bins out: Wednesday – clean the house, and so on.

That's absolutely fine by me. Most of us were brought up with routine so it's only natural and besides, without it – the world would probably be in a bigger mess than it is already in!

In an ideal world, simplicity would be beneficial to the smooth operation of this planet, but simplicity is quite simply wishful thinking if you're to stand any chance of seeing the bigger picture.

Then again some people opt not to see this complex, and sometimes scary, picture if it doesn't seem necessary. Probably wise if you don't have to be affected by it: just stay in the dark instead – there's less to take in if you can't see. Convince yourself that nothing matters if you want, and concentrate instead on perfecting your so-called essential routine if it makes you happy.

I've personally never been one for routine. I find it boring. I don't want to wake up every morning with the exact knowledge of how my day's going to progress. Where's the fun in that?

Spontaneity is a lot more exiting. However it can be a pain in the ass when your dustbin's overflowing because you forgot to put it out the week before, but generally I try to opt for the more day-to-day kind of living and just see what happens. I guess the answer is to find some kind of balance (or buy a calendar).

This isn't to say that I'm not confused – *that* I certainly am. Or, at least, I was still confused whilst watching TV that night, following my days work for Dad. I was too busy trying to figure out whose voices were in my head – that was confusing me. In fact that little puzzle had been confusing me for years and by then – I was no closer to finding out, either.

Maybe the book I picked up from Dad's stall might hold some answers – the one about palmistry.

'It's possible?' I thought, so I grabbed the book from the side-table, and took a comfortable position on my bed. This was to be the first time I'd attempted to read a book for years – a mission yet to be completed in my entire existence. The colourful pictures throughout helped motivate me to give this one a go.

Half way through the introduction and I was bored. I just wanted to know what all the lines on my hand meant, and particularly if there was any special line for people who can hear voices. I flicked through impatiently, trying to locate anything relevant to what I needed to know.

To be fair – at a quick glance, it did appear to be quite an interesting read. It seemed that expert palm-readers who actually practise this skilled art professionally, could gain a lot of information just by reading the lines on someone's hand.

It was fascinating: straight away I wanted to know about myself. Will I find love? Will I have any children? How healthy am I? Where do my talents lie? How can I make lots of money? Whose bloody voices can I hear? You know, stuff like that.

I got up and turned the main bedroom light on to get a proper good look at my palm and all its intricate creases. Next, I flicked through the various chapters, comparing my hands to the diagrams. It was quite difficult to determine which lines were which, but after about half-an-hour or so of intense studying, I'd got the general picture.

According to the lines on my hands, I was going to find love – great. Unfortunately however, my future wife was going to give birth to what appeared to be – fourteen girls, eleven boys and what I could only assume to be a lady-boy judging by the funny angle of the random crease.

Not only this though: the 'Line of Head' indicated that I was brain dead: the 'Line of Fate' wasn't even bloody there, and the 'Line of Life' indicated that I should have died years ago. 'Fan-bloody-tastic,' I thought, and chucked the book on the floor like all the others.

Suddenly my phone rang. I wondered who could be calling me, as I tried to find it amongst my bed sheets. Then I remembered the girl from the market – the one with no name who took my number: could she be phoning me? My search for the phone intensified in case this was so.

By the time I found the thing, my bed looked like a war zone; only to discover my mate Lewis was phoning to see if I wanted to meet up soon.

I met Lewis at a party in London years ago when I was living in Surrey. He lives near Heathrow airport and we've kept in touch ever since.

We spoke for a while, mainly about music because that's what we'd always had in common since the party and decided – considering we hadn't seen each other since I'd moved to Shrewsbury – we should get together in Birmingham for a night out. It was roughly half way for both of us and the idea sounded just what I needed. That's another thing I missed when I moved up here – Shrewsbury's nightlife leaves a lot to be desired (sorry Shrewsbury but come on – let's be fair).

I made my bed and climbed back on. It was then that I noticed the TV screen was a fuzzy mess. I grabbed the remote and tried to change channel – but just like at the bookstall – same story.

'Oh not this again,' I said to myself. 'I'm sorry I took you to the market today but please don't do this to me, okay.'

After fiddling with the buttons and banging the thing, it was – once again – a bloke in a suit – reading the news, who came to my rescue. It was a report about British troops in Iraq. However, this topic did interest me, especially with Marcus starting his basic training the following month. What was happening overseas would affect the nature of his deployment, if he was to get through the training, and I knew Marcus was determined to succeed. This was his chance to show everyone what he was made of, and follow in Alistair's footsteps.

Next was the weather forecast: tomorrow looking sunny but cold. Weather forecasts didn't interest me though. With my style of day-to-day living, I preferred the 'look-out-of-the-window' technique, which I find to be a lot more accurate, to say the least.

I decided to go down and get a snack from the fridge. Mum and Eric were still up. They were sitting on the sofa trying to figure out how to operate the digital camera. They'd had it since Christmas but were still unable to take a photo.

Even the combination of both their minds couldn't quite grasp the concept of the click button, and it was February!

I walked past the baffled pair wearing my boxer shorts: a little grin over my face as they bickered over where to put the memory card. I went into the kitchen, pulled the chunk of cheese from the fridge and made a sandwich, along with a nice cup of strong coffee to go with it. I went back through the front room to go upstairs, when Mum suddenly got out of her seat and raised the camera to her eye.

"Say cheese," she said.

"Oh come on Mum don't do that," I answered.

Over the last four years or so, I'd developed a (kind of) phobia towards cameras and had become a bit shy in the photo department.

"Just one snap," she insisted, so I stood there; cup in one hand; sandwich in the other, looking like a complete dipstick.

She was taking her time, trying to get a good shot of me in my boxers, but my impatience was building.

"Hurry up and take the damned photo will you Mum," I ordered.

"Okay then – smile." So I did and she pushed the button – but there was no flash.

"Nothing's happening Eric," she stated.

"Oh give it here Stella, I'll show you how to do it," demanded Eric.

"No I can do it thank you very much Eric," Mum countered.

"Look Stella, will you just give me that bloody camera," he insisted as he tried to grab it off her; "you haven't put the film in yet you stupid woman."

"Will you get off," she said. "I can flaming well do it, okay."

Soon an argument erupted, so I left them to it and went upstairs to eat my sandwich.

I put my coffee on the side table and got into bed. There was a commercial break on the telly. It was an advert for fly-spray. This seemed very strange being February and there were hardly any flies about, but anyway, this product claimed that with one squirt, all flies in its path would be dead in seconds.

I remember buying some of the same stuff a few summers previously when there were actually flies to spray. They didn't die in seconds though. I'd spray the room like a mad man just to make sure, only to come back half-an-hour later to find them upside down on the windowsill; spinning round in circles and buzzing their wings in some sort of epileptic frenzy. I would have to finish the job myself – it must have been torture for them.

I don't kill anything now – unless I really have to, or accidentally tread on a snail or something – you know.

The news returned after the commercials. It was the same bloke – wearing the same suit – reading the same stories.

As I looked on – the sound of Mum and Eric fighting downstairs filled my ears, as I tucked into the cheese sandwich. There was far too much pride at stake to ask me for help, and so the conscious decision to find my own place was made – way before they were to get their mitts on a bloody laptop. The sugar was going to repeatedly hit the fan when that event took place – that's for sure.

Anyway I put my cup down, got under the duvet and focused on Mr Newsreader:

'And now for tonight's top headline-
At least twenty-two people have died, and
many more left severely injured today,
after a block of flats collapsed in Surrey.
The accident happened in the early hours
of this morning, causing mayhem. The
five-storey building located near the town
centre of Croydon was left in ruins after
the accident at roughly six a.m. today.
Fire and ambulance crews arrived at the
scene within minutes following a
bombardment of emergency calls made
by the public. It's too soon to say at this
stage what caused the accident, but early
indications show that a possible structural
flaw could be to blame. We will now take
you live to the scene, with our
correspondent – Martin Georgiao. This

report does contain scenes which some
viewers may find disturbing.'

My eyes converged in total amazement with those of
Mr.Georgiao, as he stood in front of this mound of concrete –
talking me through the day's events. Behind him were
firemen, along with volunteering members of the public,
desperately pulling away at the vast heap of rubble, in the
bleak hope of locating any survivors.

I didn't recognise the fallen building – probably
because it wasn't there anymore. But in the background
towards the left-hand side, I could vaguely recognise a
children's play park in the dull surrounding light. It looked
exactly the same as the one next to the flat where Toby and I
used to live – surely not!

Despite impulsively thinking that such an occurrence
couldn't really be happening; the overhead view that followed,
confirmed my underlying suspicion that it was in fact – our old
block of flats.

By studying the aerial footage filmed from the
helicopter, I was able to make out the tram stop up the road,
the children's park and the neighbouring buildings. I could
even pinpoint the fish and chip shop a few hundred yards
away, next to the laundrette. It was a complete disaster zone.

I couldn't help but stare, uncontrollably, at the screen,
in a state of disbelief as to what I was seeing. The more I
stared – the more apparent it became. There was no doubt
whatsoever – that was the flat!

Previous thoughts of Lewis, Mum and Eric arguing,
the girl with no name, and my cheese sandwich were all
eradicated instantly; my mind bringing up old memories of
Croydon, Toby, and my life back then.

Questions and concerns flooded my head, which was
beginning to work overtime. How did this happen? Was
anyone I know injured? Does Toby still live there? Was he in
the flat when it happened? What if I still lived there? I could be
dead – should be dead! The line on my palm even said so!

I jumped off the bed and ran downstairs.

"Mum, Mum have you seen the news?" I shouted
before even reaching the bottom.

I burst into the front room like a crazy man struggling
to even breathe!

"Whatever's the matter with you Will?" Mum asked; both Eric and herself looking at me like I was some sort of imbecile.

"The news – have you seen it?" I tried to say whilst gasping for air.

"What about it?" They replied, almost in unison.

"The block of flats in Croydon," I prompted.

"Yes I saw that William," she acknowledged in this meaningless tone; "what about it?"

"That's where I used to bloody live Mum!"

"Oh really – well fancy that then," she replied without any apparent concept of the relevance of this freak event. Eric stunned me further, when he opened his randomly gibbering cake-hole and enlightened me with the good news:

"Well it's a good job you don't live there anymore then, I must say Will."

"That's just it," I said.

"Just what?" said Mum.

"I should have been living there but I was told to get out!"

"Oh yes – so who told you that then, love?" queried Mum, still utterly oblivious to what I was trying to explain.

"The voices, Mum – they were warning me about this!"

"Oh don't be so ridiculous William, it's just a coincidence that's all."

That was Mum's way of settling the discussion.

"Willy, we've been through this a thousand times before," interrupted Eric. "The voices are not real, and the sooner you get that little fact into your warped head – the better!"

I looked at them both as they sat complacently on the sofa, the same way they sat on the damned thing every evening, mesmerised into a zombie pose of pseudo-superiority.

Not me though. My eyes were wide open towards this one. To me, this was clearly way beyond just another evening, but instead of the ounce of understanding I so desperately needed; I ended up receiving the quick and easy overrule card that they played so frequently when faced with one of my (to them) deluded theories.

"Are you taking your tablets properly, William?" Mum asked, this being a question I would constantly be nagged with at times like this.

I retreated swiftly.

"Tell you what – forget the bloody tablets, they're good for sod all. I know what's what, okay?' I blasted angrily, and stormed up to my room.

I got back into bed feeling disappointed. That's how it worked though: the more I tried to convince people that the voices were real; the crazier people imagined I was.

The news was back to the same Iraq story so I turned over. My TV was working fine again now. After it failed on me in the market earlier, I couldn't help but get the feeling that someone purposely wanted me to watch the news that day. Was this a coincidence too? I don't think so.

I wanted to get in touch with Toby and make sure he was okay, but I'd left my mobile at the (now destroyed) flat when I desperately rushed to get out in a panic. He probably wouldn't have the same number now anyway. I concluded the best thing to do would be to phone up my old workplace and see if he was still employed there. It was getting late now, so I decided to wait till the morning.

That night – I barely slept.

Next morning was windy and wet – so much for last night's weather forecast. I eventually got out of bed and did the usual morning thing. You know: shower, teeth, breakfast, coffee and another coffee.

Mum and Eric had left early to go to the local Sunday market. They made this weekly trip religiously, every Sunday without fail. It was an alternative to church, yet they did go there to pray – pray for a bargain.  Even if there was nothing they really needed, they had to buy something, anything as long as it appeared to be a good deal. This stuff would usually then end up in the garage and Eric would spend the next week tidying it up ready for the next Sunday. After about six months or so, there would be no choice but to put on a car boot sale – it was a vicious circle.

It was nearly half-ten when I'd remembered about the block of flats collapsing (the voices reminded me). It seemed so surreal and I couldn't help but think what might have happened if the voices had never materialised.

I was happy living there with Toby, and happy in my job too. My prospects were looking good so why wouldn't I still be there? Plus, the building collapsed on Saturday morning. I always worked Friday nights and had the next morning off. It all seemed to fit together. The voices had saved me – I was convinced – but why?

More importantly – was Toby okay? I needed to find that out urgently.  It would be terrible if something bad had happened. After all, he was my best mate back then.

I got the number for 'The Lodge' from directory enquiries. Asking the man over the phone for that number felt strange, hearing it being read out by an automated voice felt even stranger. It felt like I was delving into dangerous territory, a chapter in my life that had been put to rest – besides the voices that is.

It took three attempts to dial the number without hanging up.

'Come on Will you're being stupid, just dial the number,' I encouraged myself.

I slowly entered the digits and took a deep breath:

"Hello – The Lodge – how can I help you?"

I paused.... I would have recognised that rustic voice anywhere. It was Cioffi – without a doubt. I froze – didn't know what to say.

"Hello, can I help you?" he repeated.

"Is umm Toby there please?" I asked timidly.

"Toby?  Who's Toby?" he said.

"He was one of the chefs. I was just seeing if he still worked there."

"Oh you mean Toby, I see. Toby's, well, Toby's not with us anymore, sadly."

My jaw dropped and my heart sank. I nearly dropped the phone too. I knew what was coming next, but still – I needed to hear him say it:

"Toby's actually gone and left me the rotten bugger," said Cioffi.

"What do you mean he's left you," I asked.

"Oh he took up an offer for a head chef's job in the town centre somewhere," he explained.

"A head chef's job?" I said, "What – Toby?"

"Yeah some flash git come round here and offered him more money," he continued.

"Are you sure we're talking about the same Toby?"

"There's only been one Toby. The little rascal even took off with one of my best waitresses," he informed me.

"Ah yes – that's him," I said. "Do you know if he's still alive by any chance?"

"You what? Of course he's bloody alive – that's till I get my hands on him anyway."

"Any idea where he's living now?"I asked, (and this was the key question).

"Yeah, him and his fancy piece bought a little two-bedder down West Croydon somewhere – why?"

"Oh I was just wondering, that's all."

I sighed with relief at the news he was okay.

"Anyway who is this? You sound familiar," said Cioffi.

"Umm, just a friend of his from years ago," I told him.

"I see, well if you see him – tell him I'm gonna kick his ass okay."

"Okay," I confirmed, and hung up the phone.

"You little beauty," I shouted, jumping across the sofa like a school kid on his holidays. Afterwards I just sat there in total silence – reflecting on the past. It had been the first time in years that I'd spoken to Cioffi. I couldn't bring myself to say who I was, but it still felt good – weird but good.

I started chuckling to myself. How the hell someone – who put a boiled egg under the grill – landed himself a head chef's job was beyond me. Toby's charm got him most things in life though so I wasn't that surprised really – at least he was okay.

Mum and Eric arrived about lunchtime, along with a super-mop, mini vacuum cleaner, fourteen bottles of mouthwash and a pack of 'thirty-six exposure' camera films.

They thought they'd done well that Sunday. That was until I explained that digital cameras didn't need films, but never mind hey. At least they would have fresh breath for the next few years.

I didn't tell Mum about my phone call. It would have annoyed her that I'd made the call. She saw Croydon as the place where it all went wrong for me, so she imagined there must have been something wrong with Croydon. She didn't need to know, so I just kept my mouth shut.

However she did wonder why I was in such a good mood that day. I even offered to peel the vegetables for the

Sunday roast. I didn't do the dishes though; that was Eric's job.

That night I hit the sack early. It was a tragedy that all those people had died in the accident, but, as I lay there gazing at the ceiling, I felt cheerful. My telly was working properly, dinner was delicious, Toby was okay, and I thought that I'd figured out the reason for my voices: maybe they would stop now, but not that night. They were still there for the time being. They were not really bothering me, nor did they say anything bad, but still – I could do without them.

Maybe I will wake up and they'll be gone, I hoped.

'Maybe Will – you never know. You just keep dreaming, okay mate, and I'll speak to you tomorrow.'

## CHAPTER 5

### Elusive Metal

A week had passed, but nothing had changed. The voices were still with me and Mum was still unable to use her camera. Marcus' start date for basic training was drawing closer and closer, and, to top it all off, the girl with no name had still not phoned. I was beginning to lose faith. To be quite frank, it was probably unrealistic to think that she would phone after our last two encounters: wishful thinking I guess.

Despite all of this, there were a few things keeping my spirits high. Dad agreed to put some of my pictures up for sale in his bookstall. This was a good chance to let the public get a peek at some of my stuff, and possibly get a bit of interest. Who knows? I might even sell a few. Until that point, the only pictures I'd sold were to members of my family. However these were just 'sympathy sales', and I'm pretty sure none of them have actually ended up on their walls – oh, except for Dad. He managed to find a suitable space for one of my masterpieces in his downstairs toilet. This extra loo is also the only room where Dad's girlfriend allows him to smoke.

I was also enthusiastic about the fact that Lewis and I had arranged a night out in Birmingham next Saturday. We hadn't seen each other for ages. He's a waiter in a posh hotel near Heathrow. This hotel is part of a chain. This means he was able to swindle us cheap accommodation in another hotel belonging to that chain – so that's what we planned: party till dawn and then sleep it off in style – perfect.

I never told Lewis what happened to me in Surrey, thinking he might see me as being a bit odd. He was under the impression that moving back to Shrewsbury was for financial reasons (pretty believable if you have ever lived down that end).

As far as my attitude towards the voices went, they had saved me but there was obviously more information I needed to be told; maybe a warning about another freak accident of some description, or perhaps just some general guidance on life itself. Not too sure really, but that didn't matter for now. Soon I was on my way to Brum for a night I would certainly not forget.

Saturday came and everything was set. Catch the twelve-twenty train to Birmingham New Street: meet Lewis at two p.m. in the station and check into a five (that's right – five) star hotel: hit Broad Street in the afternoon and then move onto a club later that night – I couldn't wait.

I was up early that Saturday (anticipation is a great motivator) and did my usual morning thing. Remember? Shower, teeth, breakfast, coffee. There was no 'another coffee' on this day, mind. I decided that a nice, cold, morning beer would be much more suitable. Eric was still in bed so I failed to see the harm in just having one of his tins (three if you want to get technical). I soon realised that this was most definitely a mistake and ended up having my 'another coffee' after all – before Mum and Eric came down.

I opened the living room curtains to check the weather – it was looking fair but changeable. Admittedly this method wasn't great for forecasting the weather for later that day when you're going to be over fifty miles away, but there you go. I put on some warm clothes just in case.

By the time Mum and Eric got up I'd almost got myself together again after my five percent breakfast. My wooziness was blamed on the medication – the medication that hadn't been taken. I made a promise to myself that not another drop of beer would pass my lips before meeting up with Lewis.

Later that morning, just before leaving the house, I made a final check that I had everything. My phone was fully charged: my wallet was fully loaded: I'd got spare batteries for my Walkman: spare socks and pants: train tickets and that was just about it.

"Bye Mum, bye Eric, see you tomorrow sometime," I shouted on my way through the front door.

"Oh Will, wait there a minute love," Mum shouted as she scampered down the stairs; "I bet you haven't remembered to take one of these with you."

Standing in the porch, she passed me one of my little green tablets which I stashed in that little jeans pocket where blokes keep their, umm, stamps.

"Thanks a lot Mum," I said to her, but I really meant 'thanks a bunch'. Medicine was the last thing on my mind, but nevertheless I pretended to look relieved, gave her a peck on the cheek, and headed for the bus stop.

"Have a good time Will," she bellowed down the road.

"Thanks Mum, just don't worry okay," I yelled back, but continued walking.

The Number 8 bus was roughly twelve minutes late, which was about average for round here. I jumped on and paid my ninety-five pence, (that would be inflation if you've been paying attention), and sat down.

After we rolled into Shrewsbury Bus Station I made the short walk over to the train station, only to get sidetracked by the sight of Shrewsbury Castle proudly overlooking the town below. It's a sight I'd seen many a time and I'd even been inside the castle on a few occasions to have a look at the impressive collection of military memorabilia within the Castle's War Museum. But even after the many years of living in Shrewsbury, plus the occasions when I actually visited the castle, I was still unsure who built the damned thing. As I walked with my eyes gazing up at the impressive, red-tinged, stone structure, I remembered someone once telling me that it was actually William the Conqueror who was responsible for the castle's construction. On a later occasion, when I tried telling one of my acquaintances that it was, in fact, Mr. Conqueror who set the building in motion, I was quickly put in my place and told I'd been given bogus information because W.C didn't do stone castles so someone else must have built it. You know, still to this day, that is a mystery I've never managed to get to the bottom of. Maybe you could help? Surely someone out there knows who built Shrewsbury Castle!

Anyway, after I reached the not quite but almost as impressive Shrewsbury Train Station, all I could think was 'if the little pigs built their houses out of Lego, would there be a wolf out there bad enough to blow them down?' The puzzle over the Castle had obviously deeply affected my warped little mind, to the point that momentarily I even forgot why I was at the train station in the first place (or maybe it was more to do with that alcoholic breakfast I drank earlier)!

So I stood there like a tool, for a few minutes, watching everyone else walking through the station's foyer, all clearly knowing exactly where they were going, but nobody holding any clues as to where I was going. Where was I going? Where – was – I – going? And then it hit me – hit me the way so many things hit me – Lewis!

"You're off to meet Lewis, you plum. Now get on a bloody train, and meet him before you forget. Ok, Will? Good!"

So off I went on a train, leaving Shrewsbury, its Castle, William the Conqueror, and the three little pigs behind. New programme – meet up with Lewis…

Now I know I promised not to drink any more beer before meeting Lewis, but when that drinks-trolley wheeled past my seat on the train, ten minutes after leaving Shrewsbury station – I couldn't resist.

There was motive for this however – trains put me on edge. Ever since the journey back from Croydon, there was something about trains I didn't like. It probably has something to do with feeling trapped. The noise they make, as they glide along the track, seems to somehow amplify my voices too. If there are a lot of passengers on board, it makes it very nerve-wracking when too many people are talking at once. This is why I always have my Walkman with me when travelling by train – to block them out.

Once the train left Wolverhampton, I decided I'd better ring Lewis to make sure he was en route – couldn't get through though. He was probably on his train somewhere in the countryside and didn't have any signal – so – I just put my phone back in my pocket and slowly sipped my beer. I ensured this beer lasted the entire journey too. Apart from having too many before leaving the house – have you seen how much they charge for drinks on trains?

Whilst looking out of the window at the fast changing scenery, and listening to the pumping music through my headphones, I felt the sensation that the train was going out of control. We were moving way too speedily as we passed this field full of cows on the left. I was starting to vibrate. I really was vibrating – seriously! No wait – it was my phone. That will be Lewis I assumed, so pulled out the blower and answered without looking.

"How's it going you big bald Cockney space monkey?" I said.

"Hello, is that Will?" asked this person.

It wasn't Lewis though – that was for sure. It was the voice of a girl.

"Oh sorry, who's that?" I asked.

"Don't know – you tell me," was the response, which instantly made me aware that I was actually talking to the girl I'd seen in the market a few weeks ago, whose name I'd failed to get.

"Oh I know: you're the girl I saw in the market a few weeks ago when I was working for my Dad," I said.

"That's right book-boy. So uh – what's my name then?" she tested – the answer to which I was clueless (and she knew it).

"Umm it's, it's umm – your son is called Matty and your name is umm, hang on, let me try and remember. It's umm …"

"Oh shut up Will," she interrupted me, "you didn't even ask me, you doughnut."

"Yeah I know, I'm sorry about that, how rude of me," I answered, followed by the question I'd been dying to know.

"So what is your name then?"

"Well considering you asked so nicely I'll tell you," she said; followed by a long pause of complete and utter silence.

"Hello – you still there?" I asked, but got no response.

I looked down at my phone only to see that my bloody signal had gone. This was just sensational. Now she probably thought I'd hung up on her. Surely it was game over now – I'd just called her a 'space monkey' of all the things. Not only had I humiliated myself twice in front of her, but now I'd also managed to do it from the next blinking county and still didn't know her name – great.

Luckily my phone rang again a few minutes later so I hastily answered.

"Sorry gorgeous, my signal went – I'm on a train."

"You what?" was the answer. "Have you turned gay or something?"

It was Lewis this time and now I felt even more ridiculous! Anyway it turned out that he was also on his way and everything was going to schedule.

Shortly after talking to Lewis I arrived at my destination. I took off my headphones and stepped down towards the doors before the train stopped. You can always tell when you're coming into New Street because you go through a long dark tunnel into the station (and the voice on the intercom tells you).

It was half-one: the station was rammed with noisy travellers, so my headphones were soon plugged back into my muddled ears. Lewis was due in thirty minutes so I decided to check the arrivals board and wait outside.

A little past two o'clock and so far everything had run smoothly. Lewis had arrived bang on time and we were now outside the taxi rank, wondering where on Earth our luxury hotel was. Lewis forgot to find out that little piece of information before he left. We both had bags and wanted to off-load before hitting the pop.

"Ask that Taxi driver Will, he'll know," Lewis prompted me, pointing towards this big scruffy guy with dark greasy hair, sitting in a bright pink (black) cab.

"You ask him, it's your hotel," I argued.

"That's right, so if you want to stay in the damned thing – you ask him," he demanded.

That's how Lewis operated – I could never tell if he was joking or not. There was no point in arguing so I advanced towards the 'Barbie-mobile' and stuck my head in.

After a brief discussion with Ken (who had really let himself go), the problem was solved.

"Hey Lewis, he says he will take us," I told him.

"What in that thing?" he replied. "I'm not going anywhere in that, you can forget it."

"Oh sod it, let's just get in, you wimp," I ordered, and opened the back door.

We got in and drove off. You couldn't tell that the cab was pink from the inside so it didn't really matter. What did matter was that the hotel was right behind the station and it would have been quicker to walk. The driver even charged us six pounds for his trouble.

On entering the lobby, however, all bad feelings arising from that little incident of daylight robbery were replaced with visions of gleaming marble and concierge service. Suddenly I felt like a king. Lewis had to stop me from asking one of the porters to take my bag of underwear up to the room.

We checked in and proceeded to the third floor. There was even a guy to push the button in the elevator for us – we were clearly very special people.

Down the hall was Room 304. The door was activated by some sort of credit card type of thing. It was like something I'd only seen in films. The same card turned on the lights to reveal our room – all five stars of it. En-suite bathroom – massive television – mini bar – balcony with view (well the back of the train station anyway) and a bed each, which could only be described as the most comfortable thing I'd rolled around in since my mother's womb.

After fighting for who got which bed, like a couple of juveniles, we headed into the city in search of some good bars. We ended up on Broad Street as planned, and worked our way from one end to the other.

I'm not going to bore you with the details of every bar we went in – there's too many to mention. But to give you some idea of the state we were in – by the time we got half-way down, I had somehow managed to lose the buttons off my phone, and Lewis had tried to take fifty quid out of a cash point using our hotel key-card.

Later that evening, after dining on some of the finest fast-food Birmingham had to offer, we thought it would be best to sober up a bit before trying to get into a club. This is why at the next bar we went into, we decided it would be sensible to order singles.

Now, in this place we noticed a group sitting round a table looking like they had a night of mayhem planned. The lads were in luminous clothes, face-paint, and haircuts I couldn't even begin to describe to you, with the girls in short skirts and knee-high fluffy boots.

"Will, go and find out where they're going mate," Lewis told me as we stood at the bar with our double vodkas.

"I ain't going anywhere *near* that lot mate – they look nuts!" I declared.

"Come on man, they're bound to know where the action is – look at them," he argued.

"Yeah, I can see, which is why you can ask them. Anyway I had to ask that taxi-man earlier, and look where that got us."

"Fine I'll go," said Lewis in exasperation, "you can get the drinks in instead."

He walked over to the group of 'cyber kids' and inquired where they were heading, as I ordered another round.

He came back to the bar a few minutes later with information about an all-night-rave in a warehouse just outside the city centre. Apparently there were three rooms with different music styles in each and a good line-up of DJ's. This sounded like it could be just the ticket.

"Hey Lewis, don't you need a ticket?" I asked.

"No, apparently you just pay on the door mate. Up for it?"

"Yeah, let's go for it."

We finished our drinks, plus our other drinks, and left.

It was now approaching half-nine and we thought it would be a good idea to get to the warehouse sooner rather than later, to avoid any disappointment. It was a chilly night, but as we strolled down Broad Street, the cold air seemed to keep us clear-headed. We were wondering how to get to this party.

"I don't really care how we get there, as long as it isn't in a pink cab," declared Lewis.

The chances of getting two pink cabs in one day were pretty slim, so we found a taxi rank and waited for our ride.

There was no sign of a taxi until (unimaginably) the same bloody pink one came about fifteen minutes later. We were going to walk off but I noticed that Ken must have had the night off because Barbie's bit-on-the-side was driving instead. We didn't want to wait for another so took a calculated risk and jumped in. The chances of getting ripped off by two (pink) taxi drivers in one day were pretty slim.

This bloke didn't rip us off. Instead he just didn't shut up for the entire journey. I wouldn't have minded so much, but he must have had the strongest Birmingham accent in the whole of Birmingham. We didn't understand a word. For the whole twenty minute trip, Lewis & I just sat in the back, trying to communicate with this geezer using vocabulary such as 'hmmm' and 'yeah.' When we arrived at the venue the driver asked for his fare: I had to check his meter just to make sure I heard him right.

Stepping out of the cab, the first thing you could notice was the sound of the music, throbbing through the walls of this enormous, derelict looking building. The constant thud of the baseline filled us with excitement as we joined the back of the queue. We were about ten minutes away from having a memorable night. This is how Lewis and I met – this is what we loved.

The security was on the ball at this event. The police were outside with sniffer dogs and the doormen even had hand-held metal detectors (not that us two had anything to worry about).

It was our turn to step up – Lewis first.

"Keys and mobile phones out of your pockets," instructed one of the doormen who towered over us like a beefy skyscraper.

I pulled out my keys and (now useless) phone as I watched Lewis receive the vigorous search. He was home and dry. The bouncer then looked at me and must have noticed that my eyes were a bit hazy.

"Have you got anything on you that you shouldn't have?" he asked me, to which I replied that I hadn't.

I was then instructed to raise my arms in the air whilst he ran the detector across my body. Just as the device passed down below my waist it bleeped. Great, I thought. He then started searching my pockets for what I could only assume was a weapon, but he could find no metal. I had no belt on so it couldn't be that. I even offered to lower my jeans, to show him there was no concealed machete down my pants, but he declined my invitation. Instead, he double-checked my pockets again, and this time reached deep down into my, umm, stamp-pocket to reveal one little green pill.

"What's this then?" he asked, inquisitively.

Lewis was looking back at me, probably suspecting the same thing as the doorman.

"Oh, uh it's just my medication that's all," I explained.

He clearly didn't believe me and beckoned an officer over, with his dog, to check me out.

"Come off it mate," I said; "If I wanted to come and float around your party all night, I wouldn't be taking one of them – trust me."

Regardless of saying all this, the bouncer passed the tablet to the officer while I stood there in disbelief. As the policeman inspected the tablet he clumsily dropped it on the floor next to the dog. Now everyone's eyes were fixed on the canine to see its reaction. Nothing happened. The officer gently prompted the dog by grabbing him by the collar and sticking his nose right up against the pill. The dog finally noticed the prescription drug and gave it a good sniff. It didn't stop there though. Once 'Lassie' had finished sniffing, and the officer thought he'd got a result – the stupid pooch only went and ate the damned thing.

I couldn't believe my eyes – it was so funny. The officer wasn't so amused but what could he do? Police dogs are not trained to eat class 'A' drugs, so they could only assume I was telling the truth. All I knew was that in less than an hour, that poor dog wouldn't be sniffing anything at all for a couple of days – just sleeping it off. The doorman let me through, grudgingly, and I joined Lewis.

"What was that?" Lewis asked.

"Oh, just a headache tablet," I replied. "Come on – let's party."

For the next five hours – we did.

Now that was a good night. You could always judge if it was a good night by how sweaty I got. We both came out drenched. The only thing I couldn't understand on the way back to the hotel (black cab this time) was why that metal detector started bleeping. There must be metal there somewhere or it wouldn't have bleeped – surely? Too tired to think about that at the time, all I wanted to do was get to the hotel and crash out on that super-comfy bed.

We got back and stumbled through the lobby. Having someone to push the button in the elevator really came in handy this time, but we managed to make it to our room and even opened the door.

As soon as my eyes focused on my bed that was it. I flew to it like a human magnet, muttered something along the lines of 'goodnight' to Lewis and passed out. I can only assume Lewis did the same.

Morning came for both of us in the afternoon, when a housemaid came in to clean the room.

"Oh I'm sorry," she said. "I didn't know that anyone was in here."

I looked up at her from under my duvet, wondering who the hell she was and wondering where the hell I was!

The girl left as quickly as she entered, banging the door shut behind her. It was at this point that a strange whimpering sound came from the bathroom. I got up (now realising where I was) and went in to find Lewis half-asleep, lying in the empty bathtub. I turned the light on and just spent a few seconds staring at him as he lay there, fully clothed in a bath full of air.

"Lewis! Lewis! Get up," I said, flicking the light off and on to try and bring him round.

It was extremely tempting to just turn the taps on, but I didn't have the heart to do it. Instead I just grabbed his arm and pulled him to an upright position. He sat there for a minute, rubbing his eyes and collecting his thoughts before finally touching down on 'planet reality'.

"What time is it?" He asked me.

I pulled out my phone, which made me realise two things. Firstly – it was two-thirty, and secondly – I didn't have any buttons left.

Lewis quickly shot to his feet as if he'd been given an adrenaline injection straight to the heart.

"Sugar sugarsugarsugarsugar," he repeated. "We should have checked out by twelve!"

"Oh, is that why some girl just came in to the room then?" I asked.

"Oh please tell me you're joking," he said.

He was clearly worried about creating trouble in case it got back to his boss back home.

That's one thing I admired about Lewis; the fact that he liked to party as hard as the best of them, but took his job seriously at the same time (he reminded me of myself once upon a time). As it happened, the room wasn't trashed and we hadn't caused any disturbance so it was all rosy.

We smartened ourselves up, grabbed our belongings (plus a few extras (don't tell Lewis)) and checked out. It was Sunday but the city was still vibrant (unlike sleepy Shrewsbury). Lewis wanted to have a look around a few shops before making the journey back home. I tagged along but to be honest, my mind was elsewhere for the rest of that afternoon.

A few CDs and a pair of trainers later, we went to the pub for one last drink, before going our separate ways. Lewis' train left at around six, but I knew my train ran pretty regularly so decided just to take potluck when to arrive at the station. If worst came to the worst, there was always the station pub to wait in. As it went, I just left when Lewis caught his train – a good move considering mine was just starting to board. We said our goodbyes and parted company.

I spent the entire journey home looking out of the window with my music on. The voices were louder than normal and even my headphones were ineffective at blocking them out. This was due to the fact that there was something on my mind – the mysterious metal picked up by the detector. What could it be? Were the voices trying to tell me? If there was nothing in my pockets, and no belt, then where was the metal? Was there something inside me – a device of some description?

After contemplating all the possibilities, I had reached my conclusion. That was it! That's how I could hear the voices! That's how people could monitor my every move! There was some sort of apparatus inside me that could somehow achieve this. I know it sounds farfetched but with technology these days – anything could be possible.

This was a valid explanation. Something like that must consist of metal components. As far as energising the thing – natural body heat and motion would be ample to power something that must be relatively small. But how did it get there? Who put it there? When did they put it there? Where is it exactly?

I know I said it was good news that Toby wasn't involved in the accident back in Croydon, but suddenly I felt this bitter hatred towards him. My mind told me that he was the prime suspect! We were such good friends, and now it looked as if he'd betrayed me. How could he do it to me?

There wasn't much I could do about it on the train, but it suddenly felt like there was light at the end of the tunnel. I was (in principle) sitting with my voices, and I felt more personally aware who they were. It wasn't a pleasant feeling to know something was inside me, but at least it was a solvable problem.

How it got there was a mystery. Maybe I swallowed it and it got stuck. Toby could have planted it in my sausage and mash, or something. Perhaps it was so small that it was injected into me whilst I slept, or, as a worst case scenario, someone had stuck it where the sun doesn't shine! All there was left to do, now, was prove to Mum and Eric that this is what was happening.

Later that night at Mum's, we were all sitting in the front room watching television. There was a programme on about mental illness in the U.K. Mum and Eric were engrossed, but I was just staring at the screen, trying to figure out a way of revealing to them both that, actually, I'd figured out what was going on.

They would take some convincing. There was no way they'd believe there was something implanted inside me. They would probably be annoyed if I told them, and would suggest not going out on any more wild nights.

A lot of what was said on the television programme did sound familiar, but it didn't resonate with me. I thought back to when I was first diagnosed with the illness, being shown around a day centre where I could intermix with people in the same supposed boat. That little tour further confirmed my impression that there was nothing wrong with me. I knew, just by looking around, that I definitely did not belong there. And besides – I'd made a 'mental note'.

Suddenly the answer came to me – it was so, so simple. Now all I needed to do was pluck up the courage and ask:

"Mum."

"Yes love."

"There's something I need."

"Oh yes, and what's that then love."

"Well – don't go crazy or anything but …"

"But what, William?"

"I need an x-ray."

"What do you need an x-ray for?"

"There's something inside me and I need to know what it is."

"Something like what inside you?"

"I'm not sure exactly, but it's metal."

"Has this got something to do with your voices love?"

"Well sort of – I think."

"Willy, you have got to stop this nonsense, there's nothing inside you okay."

"But Mum,"

I told them about the previous night's events, but even with this evidence – they thought I was nuts. It was probably bad timing to ask them whilst they were watching a TV programme about mental health, but this riddle needed to be solved as soon as possible. Unable to get any joy out of those two, my only option was to solve it myself.

That night I could sense a certain anxiety in the voices, as if I'd found them out. My views had dramatically changed since yesterday. They might have saved my life, but now they were just taking the piss. All this time they had been watching me, but for them it was just funny. Not for long though. Now it felt like I was in the driver's seat, and I was the one in control. Soon the fun would be over for good and I could have my life back.

I went upstairs to bed and concocted my plan against them.

## CHAPTER 6

## Charity Shop shopping


March 5, 2005. Nine days left before Marcus' basic training began. Eight days since meeting Lewis in Birmingham. Seven days since I'd figured out how I was hearing the voices. Six minutes away from phoning my psychiatrist to book my x-ray, and fifteen minutes away from being told that this was not going to be possible.

I was about to lose my temper.

"William there is nothing there, I promise you."

"Listen mate, there is something there the bloody metal detector went off okay."

"It was probably just your belt or something."

"I wasn't even wearing a bloody belt!"

Well it must have being something in your pocket then."

I checked my pockets a thousand bloody times pal: I'm not thick!"

Well I don't know but there's nothing inside you okay."

"Listen, there – is – a – thing – in – side – me – and – I – want – it – out – please!"

"Are you taking your medication properly William?"

"Oh piss off medication."

"William, I will not tolerate being spoken to like that young man."

"Okay I'm sorry, but you have to believe me – there's something there."

"Do you have any idea how many of the people I treat tell me the same thing?"

"I don't really care: I know it's there."

"Look, you're not going to convince me to let you have an x-ray, so just forget it."

"Oh come on mate?"

"No."

"Please?"

"I'm sorry. Besides, x-rays are not good for your health."

"Neither is having some sort of metal thing stuck in your body!"

"Goodbye William."

"Oh come on."

"Take the tablets, okay."

"Please? I'm begging you."

"Take care of yourself."

"Fine – well screw you then!"

"Thank you – goodbye William."

"Well, when I find out there is something, I'm going to sue your ass, okay mate! Hello? Hello? Asshole!"

To say I was disheartened would be an understatement. The shrink had got me vexed. He had managed to prevent me from resolving my issues, without batting an eyelid, and the bloody idiot was supposed to help people!

The worst thing was that now, the voices were laughing at me. It was as if they thought they'd got away with it, and were free to maintain their little charade. I was no longer in the driver's seat, but back out of control. It was like a game of tennis and the ball was once again – in their court.

There was no other way I could prove to people that something was there, and I really wasn't crazy. I needed that bloody x-ray: an x-ray looked unlikely. How else was I supposed to convince people? What was it going to take?

Suddenly my phone rang. My initial thought was that Professor Smart-Ass had come to his senses, changed his mind and realised that I wasn't cuckoo after all. But no – he hadn't – it was my dad.

"All right Dad," I answered, in a saddened tone.

"Boy you sound cheery Will," said Dad.

"Well, I'm okay," I said, "just having a bit of a bad day, that's all."

"Oh well," he sympathised, "I bet this will cheer you up."

He proceeded to tell me about this bloke who showed up at the market to enquire about a book of some description, and who took quite a liking to my artwork.

It turned out that the geezer was actually the owner of a trendy little wine-bar up town. Not only did he purchase one of my pictures, he also wanted to exhibit them in his bar, which was due to reopen in a couple of weeks following a refit.

It was crazy: they'd only been up a fortnight! Five minutes ago, I was down in the dumps, and now – there was light at the end of the tunnel (well – sixty quid for the painting anyway). Dad had also managed to sell quite a few videos over the past few weeks, so it was time for me to stock up again.

This meant charity shops.

Firstly, collect my proceeds from Dad's, and then find out more about this wine-bar caper.

It was just past lunchtime when I headed into town. I'd put aside my thoughts about x-rays and what have you, instead focusing on the more positive aspects of my life.

I left Dad's bookstall with a nice wad of cash in my pocket, plus the number for the possible future home for my pictures.

I was thrilled to say the least. This bar was right in the town's centre. It was one of those tapas joints, where only the wealthy, upper class members of the town went to wine and dine. I didn't have a clue what it was like inside – never been in before. Still, I saw this as a golden opportunity to reach an audience with big bank accounts and full pockets (not that it's about the money of course).

I left the market and went shopping – charity shop shopping.

Let me say something quickly here. You've all probably heard the saying '*Life's like a box of chocolates*', yes? Well I feel that the same is true for charity shops. That's why I like shopping in them: you never know what you're going to get.

Years ago, a person would be seen as a low-grade human being for even entering such premises. But attitudes, like most things, change. With more and more charity shops popping up in towns and cities, more and more people are realising the advantages of such outlets (mainly that everything is so cheap). It is also nice to buy something from a charity shop, because your purchase comes with the free 'feel-good' factor that flows from doing something charitable – especially if you're not normally all that charitable. I mean really – who cares if that jumper has been worn by someone else? If it looks good and it costs next to nothing, then why not?

Dad buys a lot of his books from such shops, as I buy my videos. Dad refers to it as the 'thrill of the chase,' meaning that the next rare first edition could be just around the corner. I know exactly where he's coming from, but I've never come across a video worth thousands – are there any?

Didn't find any in the first, second or third shop I went into that day, but in the fourth one I did find something a little bit more than I bargained for.

Whilst rummaging through the video shelves for some classic cinema, I could hear a gentleman at the counter enquiring as to the cost of an item in the window. I'm not sure why, but I was intrigued to discover what it was. Whatever it was cost thirty pounds, which increased my interest to know what item could be so expensive in a so-called charity shop.

At the geezer's request to view the item, I found myself moving away from the video section, and over to a shelf next to the counter to get a closer look.

As I stood in position next to the man in question – I had one eye on his own business, and the other on some horrible vase in my hand, pretending that I was some sort of antiques dealer. The trumpet-blowing little cherub painted on the vase certainly wasn't fooled.

The cashier left her post to fetch the item from the window display, and returned with a long, rectangular, cardboard box. When she placed the box on the counter, its contents still remained unclear. I shuffled across a touch to get a better view, still clutching the little cherub as my prop.

When the inquiring shopper actually opened the box to reveal its contents, I suddenly felt that all life's problems had been solved in the wink of an eye.

So what was in the mystery box that was so appealing to my needs? So much so, that as soon as I realised what it was, I dropped the vase and smashed the farting cherub to smithereens?

I'll tell you what it was – a metal detector: a bloody metal detector. The answer to my prayers: the key to the x-ray room: the big 'up yours' to my psychiatrist and every other non-believer: the end to my needless suffering: the nail in the coffin for my voices: a bloody metal detector – I'm telling you!

A quick mental calculation and assessment of the current situation prompted me to make this crucial purchase:

videos would just have to wait as I stepped across the shattered vase and butted in next to the man at the counter.

"Sorry mate – that metal detector – I need it – how much? – Thirty quid? – I'll have it – forget the bag – here you go – thanks a lot – sorry mate – I need it – thanks – sorry – bye," and off I ran.

"Hey what about the vase you broke? That was an antique you know!" the cashier called after me, but it was too late. I was already in the pound-shop buying batteries for my new device.

'Why the hell didn't you think of that sooner?' I thought. 'That's how you found out in the first place you docile plum.'

I couldn't wait to get home and prove to everyone that they were all mental, and I was the one who was fine and dandy, but the fear that they were all right and I was wrong, remained partially lodged in the back of my mind.

Only one way to find out – strip off and run the base of a great big metal detector across my naked body: beep beepbeep = metal: silence = mental.

That afternoon I stayed in my room. Mum was in the kitchen, cooking her infamous liver and bacon casserole, while Eric was in the sitting room, trying to get some sort of picture on their most recent purchase – a digibox (he's a sucker for a challenge).

Mum had regularly been cooking the same vile casserole since I can remember, despite the constant attempts by me and Eric to subtly guide her away from doing so. The screwed up faces – the eating only the potatoes – the 'Mum I really can't eat this shit' – the running to the bathroom with puffed out cheeks: all these techniques failed to eradicate this repulsive dinner. Eric and I could picture Mum in the kitchen on these particular days, laughing her ass off at her own antics. She must have known we both hated it; we couldn't have made it any clearer. I doubt she cared, considering her plate was always gone in sixty seconds, followed by her wolfing down the inevitable scraps on both of ours.

She is a good cook however: so is my Dad. That's probably where my interest in food came from in the first place, and believe it or not – I actually like liver. I could never understand how Mum could take such a succulent piece of meat, put it in a pan, and turn it into this sort of bubbling, king-size puncture-repair kit! Sorry, Mum – I love your food – but that one wasn't good (dreadful!).

Anyway, dinnertime came, and, in his 'you know what's coming' tone, Eric called me down. Normally I wouldn't be in any kind of rush to get to the dinner table – and this was no exception.

However my entrance into the dining room was a little different. Instead of just sitting down, fully clothed, in front of my mound of burning rubber, I entered, totally unfazed by the horror on my dinner plate, dressed down to my boxers, holding three and a half feet of fully charged metal detector.

The liver was not up for discussion.

"Willy, what on Earth are you doing?" asked Eric.

"Are you two ready to be educated?" I responded, with a giant smirk.

Eric looked deeply concerned, but Mum just looked like she wanted to dig into her steaming tyre.

"Today is the day that I – William the Conqueror – will remove all doubt from people's minds – by showing the nation that I am God – and can rid myself of these horrible people who are watching me – forever and ever."

"Willy, have you completely lost your marbles?" Eric responded.

"Willy, just sit down and eat your dinner please, it's going to get cold," requested Mum.

"Dinner can wait Mum," I answered, "and no, Eric, I haven't lost my marbles, as I am about to demonstrate."

"Well, this I've got to see," Eric insisted, clearly agreeing with me that dinner could wait.

I turned on the detector, picked up a fork off the table, and waved it across the base, so as to indicate that this device was the real deal.

"Absolutely brilliant William," applauded Eric, "a metal detector that detects metal – genius."

"Yeah, yeah that's right Eric, so how the fuck do you explain this?"

I grabbed the bottom of the device and pressed it firmly against my left hip: beep beepbeepbeepbeepbeep …

"Go on then Eric," I ordered, "you just tell me exactly why this thing is picking up metal in my fucking hip then. Go on – tell me!"

"Willy, please sit down," requested Mum, "I've cooked us all a lovely dinner tonight so please let's not spoil it."

"Mum – are you for real? There's something in my hip that's allowing people to watch me, and you're expecting me to sit down and tuck into yet another unwanted dose of your poisonous casserole – have a day off."

"Well what the fuck do you want me to do about it boy?" Mum asked angrily, this probably being only the third time she has ever sworn in front of me.

"I need a bloody x-ray Mum, okay!" I shouted.

The way Mum was talking it sounded like she knew exactly what was in my hip – it even sounded like she was part of the plot.

I just stood and stared at the boggled couple, who were both lost for words at my shocking discovery.

"Well, thanks for your support you two," I snapped. "I knew I could count on you."

I left the dining room, minus the metal detector, giving the pair something to think about as I went back to my bedroom. At least that little charade had got me out of dinner. Mind you, food was the last thing on my mind: people were watching me – it was official.

I could hear the panic in my voices, too. They knew the severity of the trouble they were going to get into, after I'd managed to bring a long overdue halt to this endless and damaging joke they were playing on me. Enough was enough.

Even more upsetting to me, was the sheer lack of support I received regarding the whole situation. I could have forgiven anybody for not believing me: the odds of such an event occurring are pretty slim, but now I'd given Mum and Eric proof in virtual black and white – the pair still seemed more interested in maintaining peace at the dinner table.

You can't really blame me for feeling a little dismayed, when a piece of solid liver gets a higher priority than a possible solution to my ongoing state of mental confusion, a state which had being ruining my life for years.

At least they didn't insult my intelligence too much by telling me to take my tablets properly. That would have really hurt! In fact if that had been the case, I imagine my solid piece of liver would have ended up being launched straight through the glass of the dining room window. The liver was probably even hard enough for Mum to go outside later, and find the thing using my metal detector!

That night I just lay on my bed: I didn't even get undressed. The television remained on stand-by as I gazed up in silence at the grey cloud, hovering above my head. It didn't even matter that people were watching me. Within an hour of lying there, the voices returned to their usual, nasty selves – but this didn't matter either. They could say what they want – I really couldn't care. I felt – nothing.

Just before half ten, a silver lining appeared over the grey cloud above, when my bedroom door suddenly opened to reveal the glare from the landing light, and the warming tone of my mum's voice:

"Don't worry Will, if it's an x-ray you want, then that's what we will do. I'll get it sorted for you I promise – tomorrow okay. Goodnight son."

I didn't respond but the weight had been lifted. Mum quietly closed my bedroom door, taking the silver lining with her. I was now lying in comfortable darkness. The blackness of my bedroom numbed my senses, and soon – I was asleep.

## CHAPTER 7

### Is this my Mental?

It's Thursday today: that's good enough. I don't live in Croydon anymore: that's all you need to know. I remember last Thursday – not much happened really. According to the calendar in the Chinese takeaway I'm standing in, it will be Thursday in exactly one week's time. I'm not too sure if I will be doing anything exciting next Thursday – who knows?

There's nothing special about this Thursday mind: I'm just standing next to a great big fish tank, waiting for my food. The fish seem happy enough, gliding from one side of the tank to the other. I'm watching them swim back and forth, as they move their lips like they're trying to speak.  Maybe they are – someone is.

It's Thursday and I should be happy. In a matter of minutes, a friendly Chinese girl will present me with Shrewsbury's finest sweet and sour chicken balls, which taste so good – you could eat them! I'm going to eat them all – every single one. That's why I'm here – I'm hungry.

Well, two minutes ago I was hungry anyway: now I'm not so sure. I'm not really thinking about food anymore, because two minutes ago something changed. Nothing changed really, but in my mind – it did.

So what didn't change then? Why is it that two minutes ago I was picturing myself dunking a crispy chicken-ball into a tub of red, gooey sauce, and now all I want to do is make my excuses, get back home to safety, and get away from this unclear but immediately present danger?

People are talking: I can hear them. You can't – but I can.

That friendly Chinese lady who took my order, is now my enemy. She is in the kitchen, talking to the chef about me: laughing at me and my hilarious situation. They know what's going on: they won't tell me though – it's far too funny.

Listen:

"*Oi, Will, you don't have a clue mate.*"

"What do you want?"

"*Just wanted to mess your head up for a bit, if that's okay.*"

"I just want to get my food and go home, if that's okay."

*"Can't do that, sorry."*

"Look – I haven't done anything to you, so just leave me alone."

*"Oh you're funny Will – we just want to watch you eat your chicken balls."*

"Why would you want to do that then?"

*"Because you're a dick-head and you deserve it."*

"I haven't done anything wrong for ages."

*"Can't you remember what you did you idiot?"*

"When?"

*"You dick – all the time."*

"How can you say that: you're fucking my life up."

*"Fuck off, you love it."*

"How can you say I love it: can't you see what you're doing to me?"

*"We don't really care – it's funny."*

"Well you're sick then."

*"You're the sicko: you're the one eating chicken-balls, you freak of nature."*

"They're nice."

*"Ha haha, have you heard that twat? He likes eating chicken-balls!"*

"They're not really chicken-balls."

*"Shut up you idiot: you don't even deserve them."*

"I haven't done anything wrong."

*"Yeah well, I hope you choke on them you fucking slag."*

"Why don't you just fuck off and leave me alone!"

*"What did you just say?"*

"Just leave me alone, you knob heads."

*"Oh you've had it now you cheeky prick."*

"Haven't you got anything better to do than mess with my head?"

*"Nah, this is far too entertaining."*

"Well you're just sad then."

*"You're the one talking to yourself in the fucking Chinese you prick."*

"Why are you doing this?"

*"I told you – it's funny."*

"Ha hahahaha."

"*Yeah it is ha fucking ha, isn't it!*"

"You must be really sad to spend all your time, watching my life."

"*It's not just us: there's plenty of people watching in the pub.*"

"What pub?"

"*Loads of them – you stupid twat.*"

"Yeah, so why doesn't anyone tell me then?"

"*Oh my God, he really doesn't have a clue what's going on, does he?*"

"Nothing's going on – you're just in my head."

"*What? Have you heard this dick?*"

"Shut up, shut up, shup up, shut up, shut up…"

"*Nobody's saying anything you idiot – only you.*"

"Look, I just want to get my food, go home, and eat my balls – no – sorry…"

"*Ha haha, he wants to go home and eat his balls, the dirty bastard.*"

"No, I meant…"

"*Shut up you dick: you want to eat your balls!*"

"No I don't."

"*Yeah you do, you freak.*"

"Fuck off!"

"*Temper temper.*"

"Just leave me alone now, please."

"*No.*"

"Fine then: keep destroying my life."

"*Oh come on Will – we're only having a laugh.*"

"Well, it's not funny yeah."

"*Yes it is.*"

"IT'S NOT!"

"*Shut up, you dick!*"

"Sorry."

"*Yeah well – it's a good job you make us laugh so much.*"

"Well that's okay then: at least you're enjoying yourselves."

"*Fucking too right we are.*"

"Yeah well, when I find out what's going on – you're going to be in so much shit!"

"*He has got a point Toby: we have been pretty naughty.*"

"What? Is Toby there?"

*"Shhhh, don't tell him I'm here."*

*"Fuck him Toby: let him suffer."*

*"I can't man, he used to be my mate."*

*"So what?"*

*"Yeah, but he hasn't done anything wrong, really."*

*"Yes he has: he's a dirty bastard."*

"Toby, Toby – what's going on?"

*"Oh for fucks sake, I'm going."*

"Toby, please talk to me."

*"Oh piss off you twat: Toby isn't here."*

"I just heard him talking though."

*"That wasn't Toby: just another bloke who wants to kick your head in."*

"Well tell him to fuck off then."

*"Oh you're in so much trouble Will: I feel sorry for you."*

"Why?"

*"I don't really you idiot: you're just an idiot."*

"How can you judge me when you're doing this to me, you dicks?"

*"Ooohh, dicks are we?"*

"Well what do you want me to say?"

*"Just say anything: you're making us laugh."*

"Yeah well, you're fucking my life up."

*"Ah, poor Will. Don't worry – it will all be over soon."*

"When?"

*"I don't really know: a few more years yet, sorry."*

"The trouble is that I keep hearing the same old shit."

*"Well it's not really up to you, is it Will?"*

"Oh just shut up: you're not even real."

*"Whatever."*

"Not real!"

*"Yes we are."*

"Not real!"

*"You're such a dick."*

"Not real, not real, not real, not real, not real…"

*"Enjoy eating your balls you dick."*

"One chicken-balls, one egg-fried rice, and two spring rolls?"

"Oh thanks, that's me."

"Here you go: enjoy your meal, sir."

"Thanks a lot."

"Thank you, good bye."

"Bye."

'What the hell just happened? That Chinese girl seemed friendly enough after all.'

It's Thursday today, and everything's fine again. The sun is shining and my chicken smells lovely. Boy I'm hungry.

**Interlude**

*'Lemonade'*

I love talking about myself – it's great. If I had my own way, this book would be all – 'me memememememe.' However, I do appreciate the fact that all this self-talk will probably start to get on your nerves if I carry on too much longer. You don't want to hear me rambling on about how I did 'this' and how I did 'that' and then I said 'this' and so on. This is why I've decided to give you a short break where we can discuss a different topic.

Instead, how about I explain to you the ins and outs of basic home decorating? No – too boring. Okay then, maybe a quick and simple explanation of algebra? Nah – too intellectual. (I don't even know anyway.)

Tell you what – go and grab a cup of coffee, come back, and I'll give you a brief summary of the history and effects of amphetamine – that'll do. Can you make me one while you're there? Two sugars please – thanks.

Right then: the word 'amphetamine' is derived from the chemical name of the compound alpha-methylphenethylamine! Amphetamine is bad enough, so for the sake of simplicity, I will just refer to the stuff as speed.

Now 'speed' is a synthetic manufactured product, which was first produced in the 1880s by some German geezer. It was used medically as a stimulant, and also as a tonic for suppressing the appetite.

This was soon recognised by military authorities all over the world. The drug was given to troops who were engaged in battle, or when long periods without food were required. During World War II, British troops were getting pumped full of the stuff to keep them alert during the conflict.

Since the 1950s especially, more and more people have become conscious of their weight in a world where the slimmer body has become more and more fashionable. For this reason, huge quantities of the drug have been prescribed to these people as a means of weight loss. However, this is risky business and has now pretty much ceased. In the 1970s it became illegal, and was categorised as a class 'B' drug.

Despite all of this, people have had their own ideas about the potential of the drug and, today, the recreational use of speed has spawned an illicit and very lucrative industry. Like I said, it was created in Germany and yet, with a bit of 'chemical know-how' and some basic tools, practically anyone can make the stuff.

So what does it do? Well, for starters – everything speeds up (hence the name). The user feels more energetic, along with having a greater sense of urgency. Self-confidence levels rise and fatigue fades, with people going days on end without sleep. The brain starts to work overtime as the mind is filled with many different thoughts at once. This usually results in the user talking a load of gibberish, but for them – it all makes sense.

People most commonly take the drug by consuming it orally. In its powdered form, the drug can be snorted to enhance and speed up the effects. There are cases when people even inject the drug straight into their blood stream. This is most definitely a foolish thing to do, considering it is almost impossible to determine the purity of the drug, resulting in a high risk of overdosing.

The drug works by stimulating the nervous system. It operates in the same manner as adrenaline. The heart-rate increases as the blood-pressure rises, resulting in the body's temperature escalating. The increased levels of energy mean that the user can sustain longer periods of physical activity (such as dancing).

But what goes up, must come down. The body has been forced by the 'lemonade' to provide extra energy, and once it is all over – that energy must be paid back. Blood sugars have been lost, as well as the body's natural salts. The user then feels lethargic, weak and tired. Feelings of paranoia and depression kick in. The body's exhausted, but the brain is still racing, so sleep becomes almost impossible.

The drug isn't addictive (strictly speaking). However, this is not to say that with regular use, the user won't reach a stage when they can't manage without it. There comes a point when the only solution to combat such intense exhaustion – is to take more. This is when major problems can surface.

Taking speed rarely results in physical problems (apart from the odd heart attack, liver or kidney failure, and bouts of unconsciousness). The general sensation of feeling 'run-down' can be dealt with by allowing the body to rest and to regain its strength naturally. The temptation to take more of the drug, allowing the user to keep going, is certainly a mistake. Also, the fact that the body develops a tolerance towards the drug means that the user needs more and more to get the same effect.

With continued or heavy use, this drug can cause profound and distressing psychological problems. Most of us probably have the potential to be able to cope with a physical illness or infirmity, but a mental illness is different. Users of this drug should realise that they are taking something that has a real potential for releasing latent mental illnesses, which may be difficult to treat successfully, if not impossible.

Depression can turn into extreme paranoia, with the sufferer feeling that everyone is against them. The user creates complicated and well-constructed delusions with beliefs that people around them are part of a complex plot to somehow destroy them. These delusions can seem like reality, and become part of everyday life (scary stuff).

In saying all of this, my advice would definitely be to steer clear of the stuff altogether. Who knows what might happen!

I just thought you might like to know – that's all.

Anyway, on that note – let's get back to the programme.

# CHAPTER 8

## The Prick of Destiny

March 6, 2005. Eight days before Marcus' basic training began. Seven days since meeting Lewis in Birmingham. Six days since I'd figured out how I was hearing the voices. Five minutes away from phoning my psychiatrist to tell him he owes me thirty quid for the metal detector, and four days away from sitting in a hospital waiting room, waiting to be cured.

Not a lot happened on March 6, so I'll skip to four days later, when I was sitting in the hospital.

It was a Thursday: I remember it well. Out of all the days I could possibly be having an x-ray, it just happened to land on that particular Thursday. You see, I wasn't the only one who was sitting in the x-ray waiting room that day, waiting to be cured. As I sat in my blue plastic chair, holding ticket number whatever, as if I was at some sort of cheese counter, guess who came and sat next to me with one arm in a sling and a seemingly hostile grin across her angelic face. I'll tell you who. Actually no – I will let her tell you herself...

"It's Jolie, you stupid moron!"

"Ah, Jolie – I see. Nice name."

"Yeah, well – thanks, I suppose."

"So I was probably way off the mark with Space Monkey then."

"Hey, shit-bag," she whispered frighteningly. "Just because you're in a hospital, don't start thinking that you're safe, okay. I've still got one arm left to slap you all the way to the morgue."

"Alright, alright, I was only joking," I said defensively, "anyway, what have you done to your arm?"

"Well if you must know, I pulverized some cheeky git to death with it."

"Oh, I see."

"Yeah, I can introduce you to him if you like."

"No it's okay," I said, "I'll be on my best behavior."

"Very wise William – very wise."

"Oh, so you remembered my name then," I replied.

"Yeah well, how could I forget such an odd creature like you?" said Jolie.

"I see, and what's that supposed to mean?" I wondered, aloud.

"Well, put it this way Will. I'd say that you're the space monkey, not me."

"Yes, so I've been told," I admitted.

"Anyway, why are you waiting in the X-ray department?" she asked, inquisitively. "There doesn't look like there's anything wrong with you."

"Ummm…"

The next ten minutes or so of conversation, which lasted until my number was called, strengthened Jolie's theory that I was, in fact, a full-blown, grade 'A' space monkey. Looking back now, I can't really blame her for thinking I was from another planet. I mean, what would anyone think if someone tried telling them that they had a tracking device planted in their hip?

Fortunately for me, however, Jolie seemed to like space monkeys, and before heading into the X-ray room, I invited her to join me at Marcus' leaving party the following night at nowhere else but *Dibdabs*. But that's another chapter.

So I left Jolie in the waiting area, having successfully learnt her name, and joined this geezer wearing a whiter than white uniform in the X-ray room. The bloke then spent a few moments poring through his notes while I stood there like a spare part; watching his face, and trying to read his thoughts.

After the doctor finished digesting his paperwork, he then introduced me to the x-ray machine which was ominously suspended above the examining table. The only thing I can remember thinking as I inspected the impressive piece of kit, was that it must have cost a bloody fortune.

Professor X then talked me through the procedure, and just as nerves took over my body, I was delighted to learn that I could actually keep my boxer-shorts on during the test.

I shouldn't have been feeling nervous anyway. I was about to bring closure to my ongoing ordeal, and prevent any more suffering being inflicted by those bloody voices.

Still, as I started to undress, the fear that I could be wrong was definitely present. There must be a limit to the amount of people who tell you that you're mental, before you start believing that you are.

One thing I knew for sure, however, was that mental or not-mental, a bloody metal-detector doesn't start bleeping just because it feels like it. So as I took up position beneath the x-ray machine, I knew that whatever the outcome - this was a procedure which needed to be performed.

And so it was done.

If you blinked then you probably missed it: I certainly did. Before even realizing what was happening, I was being ordered to put my clothes back on, and park my backside right back out in the waiting room. It was literally twenty seconds of seeming nothingness. I was at least expecting some flashing lights, or some robotic noises of some kind. But no: nothing, not even a tickle. So I was back in the waiting-room on my blue plastic chair next to Jolie. Even she was surprised how fast it had happened. She was still waiting for her own number to be called.

As we both sat there waiting, Jolie told me that she didn't really pulverize someone to death with her fist, but she had decided, however, to pick a fight with a solid door, after a heated argument with one of her sisters.

It was strange really. As I sat next to Jolie, whilst awaiting potentially life-changing news, she actually made me feel positively relaxed, despite the clear evidence that she didn't mind using her fists if, or if not, required. Despite all previous hiccups during our previous encounters, you could say that this shared twenty minutes or so, in a hospital waiting-room, seemed to connect us in a way that I'd never really experienced with anyone else before.

I explained to Jolie about my brother Marcus, and how he was joining the Army the following week, this being the reason for a leaving party.

Luckily for Jolie, her mother was looking after little Matty for the weekend, after Jolie's close encounter with a solid oak door. She just couldn't understand why it was being held at *Dibdabs* of all places (she had obviously never sat on that black leather sofa before), and yet she accepted my invitation all the same.

Anyway, Jolie's number was called mid-conversation so she told me she'd call next day to make arrangements for that evening. She then wished me luck with my – ummm – problem, and walked through to a different room with another geezer wearing a whiter-than-white uniform (it was like some sort of competition).

My attention was soon focused once more on the whole reason why I was sat there in the first place. I couldn't keep my hands still, anticipating the outcome of the x-ray and all it was going to show. Other people in the waiting area must have thought that I was practicing to become a conductor or something daft.

Roughly fifteen minutes passed before Professor X popped his head round the door and called me through. I could just tell by the soft and gentle tone of his voice, that my x-ray had come back – shall we say – 'positive'.

My heart-rate shot up as I left my chair and slowly advanced towards the x-ray room for the second time; the x-ray dude holding the door open for me. Everyone else in the waiting room just watched as I stepped past them, what with me being in apparent perfect health. I mean, everybody else was either in a sling, plaster or a wheelchair. One guy was even holding his ticket number with his teeth!

Anyway, once I was back in the examining room, Professor X told me to have a seat at the end of the table. He had my x-ray print in his gloved hand. My eyes were fixated on his every action, as he turned on the wall-screen-device-thingy (that's the technical name for it), and hung my x-ray over the light to get a clear picture.

He then turned to face me.

"Well," I said.

"Well William," he answered. "I have to say it's a pretty good job you came to see us."

"What do you mean, Doc?" I asked, inquisitively.

"What I mean William, is that you were right."

I couldn't believe what the man was saying to me. I imagine the way I suddenly felt was equivalent to the feeling of getting six numbers on the lottery (maybe even five and the bonus ball too). My face instantly lit up like the sun, as my smile expanded to my delighted ears.

"Here, let me show you on this print," the 'professor' continued.

Before taking a look, I sprung off the examining table and started bouncing around the X-ray room like a euphoric jack-in-the-box.

"Ha hahahaha, what did I say?" I shouted. "I knew I was right you dickheads. Ha haha, what are you going to do now? You've all had it now, you're all screwed – hear me – SCREWED!"

"William, William, William, calm down a bit," the doctor interrupted me. "Who are you talking to, exactly?"

"I don't know yet but I'm going to find out soon enough – CAN YOU HEAR ME YOU SHITHEADS?"

"William, William, just slow down a bit, okay," I was urged.

After catching my breath, I confidently stood there, feeling the victory pumping through my veins. All that was missing was the shiny gold medal, dangling from my neck. Unfortunately, Professor X failed to understand the nature of my victory, as, with fleeting alarm in his eyes, he glanced at me before directing my attention towards the x-ray print on the wall.

"Now then William," he began, "what you are looking at here is your pelvis."

I followed the nib of his fountain pen, as he proceeded to point out the various areas of my x-ray, and explained in simple terms what was going on, so as not to confuse me.

"And just below this part of the bone next to the surface of the skin, you can clearly see what appears to be a tiny shard of metal, or probably a pin of some description, entering your hip just here."

I moved my head up close to get a good look at the foreign object, while simultaneously trying to position my hand over the right place on my jeans, to get a better understanding of the situation.

The doctor looked at me as I pressed my palm against my hip.

"Can't you feel that William?" he asked me.

I just continued to gape at the screen, whilst silently building my own conclusions in my head. I think the doctor must have sensed that my brain was operating on a completely different wavelength than his own, and so left me to my own devices for a few moments.

A couple of minutes later and I answered the Doc's question.

"Well my hip has felt a bit weird, but that's been going on for a long time now."

"What do you mean, William? As in weeks, months?"

"Probably about ten years or so I think."

"Ten years you say!"

"Yeah about that," I said. I followed up by asking, "are you sure this is just a pin?"

"That's what it looks like to me, William," said the doctor.

"So it's definitely not a tracking device then?" I checked.

"I doubt it very much," he answered. "Here – let's take a look and see what we can see, okay."

As I once again started to remove my jeans, I felt the gold medal slip from around my neck, and crash to the floor with a great big thud. I raised the side of my boxer shorts to allow Professor X to investigate the suspected point of entry, of what was fast looking likely to be a bloody pin, after all the drama I'd created.

"It looks like this is the point right here William, see."

"What, that tiny little red pimple thing do you mean?"

"Well, according to the x-ray it would make sense."

The doctor gently pressed against the probable entry point, but all I could really feel was the same mild throbbing sensation that I'd been experiencing for the last ten years or so, ever since waking up in my bed one morning back when I was first living at Mum's.

"Well there's definitely something there William," stated the doctor, "and this is almost certainly the entry point, which means that we need to remove it as soon as possible."

As the doctor explained what would happen next, I was quickly putting the pieces of the jigsaw together in my head. Unfortunately, the picture developing was not the one I was expecting to see, and yet the pieces just fit perfectly. Another look at the object on the print-out resulted in the creation of a new theory.

Three words just kept repeating themselves inside my brain. That bloody Marcus – that bloody Marcus – that bloody Marcus.

After the simple procedure was carried out the very next morning, extracting one tiny sewing pin which could only have come from Mum's sewing kit, my new theory was now fact, and three words just didn't seem to cover it somehow.

Ten bloody years of walking around with a damned sewing pin lodged in my hip, all because my stupid little brother thought it would be funny to stick a load of pins in my bloody mattress, once upon a sodding time.

The doctors were just astonished how I hadn't noticed for so long, and how it hadn't got infected at all. I was too enraged to be astonished: I wanted blood – Marcus' blood – lots of it!

Three measly stitches later, and I was out of the hospital doors, straight into a taxi home, with exhibit 'A' secure in my wallet.

It was Friday, and guess who I'd be seeing later that evening at their leaving party? That's right – the very man himself. Basic training just didn't start soon enough. Another few days and he would have been safe, but no – he wasn't safe – far from it.

A brief scan over with the metal detector back at mum's confirmed that the metal had gone, and I was (possibly) mental.

But no, I had made a mental note that this was real, and no matter what the future might hold, I was sticking to it.

So I tried to remain unfazed by the temporary little setback concerning my voices, which, by now, were back to their usual tricks. But, as I got ready to go out that evening, my thoughts were directed at getting even with Marcus, but like I said before - that's another chapter…

**Interlude**

*'Speaking your Mind'*

So: is 'speaking your mind' a good idea or a bad idea? Well, I'm not convinced that there's a correct answer to this question really. In my opinion, every situation in life should be dealt with in a specific manner. Now if that means speaking your mind, then so be it.

This is most definitely easier said than done (excuse the apparent witticism) in my case, but I'm convinced that in certain situations, if something is on your mind, then that's where it should stay.

Are you following me so far?

I guess what I'm talking about is tact. You've got one group of people who deal with awkward situations with a certain amount of diplomacy. Then there's another group, who I suppose are of a less sensitive nature than others. And then there's Jolie, who has never even heard the word *sensitivity*, let alone possesses any!

Now this is all down to Jolie's enormous natural capacity to speak her mind. No matter what the situation, Jolie will speak her mind without giving it a second thought.

However, in my mind, speaking your mind does require a certain degree of craft or skill, especially to know when you should speak up, or sit back and shut up, which Jolie clearly doesn't.

But I do have to admit that I really admire Jolie's ability to express her thoughts without any apparent concern for the consequences such actions could cause. In all fairness, she's done remarkably well not to have ended up on a hospital operating table, or even behind bars, due to her free flowing gob, connected to her fiery-tempered brain.

Nevertheless, sometimes it is definitely correct to speak up if something is not right. So when these situations arise, Jolie handles them remarkably well.

She often urges me to do the same, and in all honesty – she's right! Speaking my mind is most definitely an area in my life that requires a touch of work. If I took after Mum in any way, then speaking my mind shouldn't be too much of a problem, considering that Mum deals with problems in a similar manner to Jolie. Possibly not quite to the same shocking and harrowing extent as Jolie manages to, but still, if you're in the wrong (or right sometimes) and Mum's about – watch out!

I remember when I was a kid. One time, Mum took me and a friend of mine to the cinema, so we could go and watch a film by ourselves, only to find the pair of us in the lobby five minutes later, nearly in tears. This was all because the ticket-checking geezer refused us entry, as we were carrying bags of sweets which were purchased from, well, not the cinema.

After I explained the unfortunate situation to my understanding mother, it turned out that my distraught friend and I were in fact allowed to take whatever we wanted into the cinema that day, and we also received a full refund for missing the first five minutes of the film.

After a proper roasting from my mum, I would imagine the bloke in question either quit his job due to trauma – *or* – developed a serious phobia about denying any child their wishes, after that pivotal day in his ticket-checking career.

Jolie doesn't always stop at speaking her mind, and sometimes lets her fists do the talking instead. This could partially be blamed on the fact that she's actually a dragon. (That's her Chinese zodiac animal by the way).

Fighting ability: another area of my life that Jolie urges me to develop. But to be honest, I am proud of the fact that I will do anything within my power to handle a situation without the use of any form of violence if possible. There are many tasks in life that I can do well with my hands, but smashing seven bells of sugar out of someone - isn't one of them.

But yes, like I said, it would be nice to be able to speak my mind a little bit more. There have been numerous occasions in the past where speaking my mind would have been the best policy. Come to think of it, sitting back and shutting up has resulted in me having to settle for second prize (in a manner of speaking) too many times, when I clearly should be walking away with the winning trophy instead.

Let me give you a classic example.

Not so long ago, I took Jolie to a luxury hotel, next to a lake in Wales, for a romantic weekend, as a birthday gift. It would probably have been more romantic if, a couple of days previously, she hadn't fallen down the stairs, cracking three ribs, as she brushed her teeth in our multi-storey house. This is one reason why there are no sex scenes in this book.

Anyway, despite that minor hiccup, it was an enjoyable couple of days away, regardless of Jolie's inability to – well – move. On the first evening, after a relaxing session in the hotel's spa, we sat down in the restaurant for a romantic five (yes five!) course dinner: something new to both Jolie and me.

Now apart from getting slightly confused by the abundance of cutlery present on our table, everything was going superbly well I have to say.

But then my main course came out. Salmon and scallops with caramelized leeks and a mustard and dill sauce. It looked lovely. It smelt lovely. My eyes were saying: "Yes please." My tummy was saying: "Feed me baby – feed me now!"

And then I tucked in. I took a bite of the perfectly cooked salmon, smothered in some of the delicately fragrant sauce, but as I started to chew, my teeth began to grind on what could only be described as sand. No – not described as sand – it was sand. And not just a couple of grains of sand either. I'm talking about half a bloody beach of sand! Jolie could hear me biting it from her side of the table as if it was a bowl of snap, crackle and pop!

Now, considering this wasn't exactly fast food (and because Jolie forced me to), I called the waitress over to express my displeasure with the quality of my dinner. And, in response to my complaint, the waitress told me she would have a word with the kitchen staff, only to come back two minutes later with the chef's side of the story.

I was told by this waitress, that the chef actually likes to grind the dill and then crystallize it to bring out a fuller flavour to complement the salmon.

So what did I say?

"Oh right – I see – thank you."

And that's it! I even expressed gratitude for being served a plate full of grit!

What I should have said, and what I wish I had said, was something along the lines of …

"Listen sweetheart, I know it's not your fault or anything, but actually I used to be a chef so I've got a rough idea of what I'm talking about, and I've never heard of 'crystallized dill'. Now I could be wrong, but even if there was a way to turn dill into crystals to enhance its flavor, why would anyone want to if it's going to make the dish feel like a sandpit? I'm not blaming you, but could you kindly take that shit away and bring me a lamb shank instead? Oh, and while you're in the kitchen, could you please tell the chef who fed you that little story about the secret crystal dill, that it was probably the most creative excuse for a crap meal I've ever heard in my life, but unfortunately it won't wash with me and tell him also, that he's making the waiting staff look like idiots – thank you."

But no – I didn't say that at all: I just put up with it. Next time I will just have to remember to bring my bucket and spade (or order something else).

So, is it a good idea to speak your mind, or not?

"Tell me – what's on your mind?"

Anyway, on that note – let's get back to the programme...

## CHAPTER 9

### *Another Chapter*

Before I get under way with this chapter, can I just take the time to enlighten you with a thing or two? Sometimes I like to consider myself a bit of a Jedi warrior. Now, before you all jump the gun and start accusing me of being crazy, I feel that it's well within my rights to believe such a thing. For starters, there are the voices. I mean, who's to say that they're not extraterrestrials from a galaxy far, far away. Who knows? Maybe they are.

Unfortunately, I don't happen to possess one of those light sabres or anything, but I do find that the remote control for the television makes a pretty good substitute. With all those channels available at the touch of a button, I definitely sense a certain amount of power when holding the TV remote. It must have something to do with being able to change channel without actually touching the TV set. You could say the same about the Jedi ability to move objects, just by using 'the force'.

Impossible you say: perhaps. But there's nothing wrong with using your imagination of course. Your imagination can set you free if you allow it to. And yet the whole concept of 'the force' is pretty relevant to how the world works. Most things in life are categorised in either a positive or negative way, in relationship to the whole: hot or cold – happy or sad – love or hate, are just a few examples of the opposites within life's spectrum.

And of course, there are both the good and the bad sides of the force too. I usually opt for the good side most of the time when in Jedi mode. However, this is not to say that I don't flip to the dark side from time to time.

The day that the doctor removed a bloody sewing-pin from my hip, (surreptitiously inserted there by dear Marcus), I was ready to give my 'little' brother a taste of just how potent the dark side could be.

To be perfectly honest, Marcus has been flipping to and from the dark side for as long as I can remember. Ever since the first time I met him, when his dad got together with my mum back in the day, all he's done is cause problems – with his sneaky antics and wild outbursts. He was still at it by the time he started growing spots on the cheeky little skull which protected his scheming mind. I remember one time, our first family holiday together (somewhere on the coast of Wales) was brought to a premature end due to Mum not being able to take anymore of Marcus' nightmarish behavior. In all fairness, he really can be bloody horrendous! Anyway, maybe the Army will sort his lid out. Miracles do happen, I suppose.

Anyway, he hadn't made it to the Army when I came out of that hospital, and I was ready to flip to the darkest dark side I've ever flipped to, thanks to this latest ordeal created by the one and only Marcus. Thank the Lord there wasn't an evil twin thrown in with the package…

After I left the hospital that Friday, I had visions of grabbing the little git, and ramming the Death Star right up where the sun doesn't shine, to see how he'd like that. *He* could then be the one sitting in a hospital waiting- room. It was a nice thought (as long as you don't think too much about it), but, unfortunately for me, Marcus was hardly 'a little git' any more. The best remedy for my damaged ego was to swallow my pride, and take a dose of 'forgiveness', whilst making light of the whole thing.

Oh well, he was about to embark on one of the most physically and mentally demanding careers going, so, to be honest, he had by that time earned my full respect. I just hoped he was doing it for the right reasons.  He always did tackle life like a bull in a china shop, and he always did feel like he had something to prove.

Not to me, though. I already knew that my little brother was a class act, and I was going to miss him deeply. Part of me didn't want him to make it through the training, but after I realised that he really wasn't happy working for his uncle, I put aside any selfish thoughts, and gave him my full blessing instead.

I still wanted to get the little rascal back for the whole pin-in-the-hip thing though. I was having trouble letting that one rest, especially after Jolie phoned that Friday, and I had to explain how my tracking device actually turned out to be a bloody pin. In fact, I had to explain to everyone that day what had really happened back at the hospital: the answer to which just completely stunned Mum and Eric beyond belief.

One positive consequence of such a bizarre event was that, ever since the pin was discovered, my psychiatrist seemed to take me a little more seriously. This was probably down to the fact that if I hadn't had that X-ray, he could have, potentially, been held responsible for any amputations that may have followed.

However, he still didn't give me my thirty quid back for the metal detector. Instead he suggested that I take up treasure hunting as a new hobby! A very brave response in my mind, considering he should have been at home rewriting the textbooks regarding the correct procedure when dealing with someone who claims to have metal in their body. Wouldn't you agree?

Another result of the discovery of the pin, was that (in a way) I'd put Mum and Eric in their place somewhat. However much it must have pained them to do so, they, too, were obliged to listen to any of my future requests and desires with a little more tolerance than before.

Unfortunately this is not to say that their views on my voices had changed much. In fact, Mum, especially, felt that the removal of the sewing pin would bring closure to the whole situation, when it really just created a whole new set of problems for me. Basically, I was back to square one!

Jolie just wanted to meet my brother and shake his hand for giving her such a laugh. It was probably a good job that my brother was left-handed, considering that Jolie's right hand was now covered in plaster. So anyway, like I said, Jolie did phone me that Friday, and after I managed not to call her a space monkey, we arranged to meet up in a quiet little boozer in town, before heading to *Dibdabs* for Marcus' leaving party.

Now at this point, let me tell you a thing or two about parties at *Dibdabs*. Basically, if you look beyond the general lack of atmosphere, the rubbish beer, and the morbid staff, *Dibdabs* is actually a pretty good venue to host a private party. Actually, it would be fair to say that a lot of Shrewsbury's party animals do tend to choose *Dibdabs* as the place to hold their gatherings.

My motto regarding parties has always been the same – who needs a reason? One thing that makes *Dibdabs* a popular location for a party is that it's potentially free to book. Basically, you have to pay a deposit of £150, which gets you your own DJ and doormen, but if more than fifty people turn up on the night, then you get your deposit back – lovely. I've always felt that there should be no deposit to pay, and if more than five people turn up, then they should be bloody grateful! But you know – rules are rules.

That was pretty much it as far as rules were concerned. I remember sometime ago, Marcus and I were having a few beers in town and we decided to phone up *Dibdabs* for a laugh and book a phantom birthday party for a two hundred strong crowd. The boss (whose name forgets me) sounded extremely excited as he explained the deposit rule to us over the loudspeaker. He was thrilled with our proposal, so much so that he wasn't even deterred when Marcus requested that we brought a selection of farm animals along for the celebrations. The only point he made about his establishment being transformed into Noah's Ark, was that no farm animal could be counted as a guest in the matter of obtaining our deposit back. I couldn't believe my ears (like normal), and neither could Marcus. The gaffer would have probably given the thumbs up to a combine harvester if only the front door was big enough!

So anyway, let's get back to the evening of Marcus' very real and completely animal-free party (well, animal-free if you exclude Marcus' girlfriend Lottie that is).

It was around half-past-seven when I left Mum's to meet Jolie in town.  The Number 8 was about twenty-five minutes late, which quite frankly took the piss! In a way though, it worked out quite nicely since Jolie's cunning plan to arrive fashionably late was foiled, as I arrived ten minutes after her.

We met in a quiet little bar, just down the road from her mother's chocolate shop (I'll get to that later), where her family usually end up in the evening for a drink after work. Luckily for me, at this early stage of romantic development, her family had not gathered there on this occasion. Instead, as I stepped through the doorway, I was faced with just a handful of drinkers standing at the bar munching on peanuts, and sitting at a table in the corner next to the fruit machine, was Jolie.

What a glorious sight to see: all those flashing lights and a thirty-five pound jackpot. Jolie didn't look too bad either. She didn't look very impressed with my time-keeping though, and that pretty black dress just didn't quite harmonize with the bright blue, fibreglass, arm-piece she had on. But apart from those few particulars, she was of course – an angel.

I walked up to her table and dumped my bulky bag (the contents of which will be revealed shortly) down on the floor. My apologetic 'smile' worked a treat, and I gratefully received my first peck on the cheek from this girl, who, by now, was inching closer and closer to becoming my fiancée – no sorry – girlfriend.

Just to prove that I wasn't completely forgiven for the late arrival, Jolie requested a double brandy and cola when offered a drink from the bar. To me, this was an early indication that there was going to be a fight for the trousers.

So, like a good little boy, I did what I was told. I went to the bar and returned with our drinks.

By half-nine we'd already sunk a few beverages and were in deep conversation, mainly about our recent hospital experiences. Jolie was such an easy girl to talk to about things. Even though she did put on this caustic front, I knew that it was just her defense mechanism and really she was genuinely open minded to my viewpoints. I certainly think she'd never met anyone else like me before. Come to think of it, I don't think I have either.

It was fast approaching ten o'clock and I started to vibrate. Jolie had just told me a joke, but no – it wasn't funny – it was my phone.

"Where the bloody hell are you?" shouted Marcus.

"Oh sorry, bruv," I answered. "We're just on our way now."

"We – who's we?" he asked.

"You know – we," I clearly explained.

"Ah, you mean you and hot stuff," deduced Marcus.

"That's the one, bruv."

"Well, hurry your asses up," urged Marcus. "We're in desperate need of some decent music here."

"Okay mate – five minutes yeah."

"Okay bruv – see you in a min."

I put the phone down and coaxed Jolie into downing her drink so we could get to the party.

It's probably an appropriate time to mention what was in my bag now. Well, I wasn't going to mention this at all but I was, in fact, carrying a selection of twelve-inches. No - not dildos - I mean records! House records to be exact – the dirtiest electro-filth imaginable to be more exact. To the older readers amongst you, that's music that goes "bang bangbangbangbang" which isn't really music at all. You know the stuff: it all sounds the same.

Yeah, you could say that, apart from the cooking and the painting, I'm also partial to a bit of the old 'spin spin' sugar too. I've even got a DJ name - Good Will Bumpin'.

It all stems from the Croydon days when I started to buy 12-inch singles, quite plainly because I was tired of buying CDs with maybe twenty tunes on them – but finding that I only liked two of them.

So I collected vinyl instead. And then, one day (my birthday), a girl I was seeing at the time bought me some secondhand turntables so I could start mixing. That girlfriend soon realized the error of her ways, and quickly became my ex-girlfriend after practically needing a crowbar to prize me away from my new toys. I was hooked, and have been engaged in a love affair with mixing ever since.

I don't want to blow my own trumpet too much, but after a while I started to get pretty tip-top on the old decks. I put this down to the fact that after my – ummm – 'accident', I found that mixing was a good distraction from the bad stuff. At the same time it also meant that even if nobody was physically present in the room, there were still my voices to hear me play. Because of the critical nature of this illusory audience, I was determined to play even better. In the end I simply refused to make a mistake.

And that's how it happened: the birth of Good Will Bumpin'.

So anyway, enough about all that, where were we? Oh yeah, so we drank our drinks and left the pub. Next stop - *Dibdabs*.

"Don't tell me that you're going to be busy playing music all night Will," said Jolie.

"No don't worry," I answered, "just a little bit."

"Oh great," she grumbled. "So what am I supposed to do?"

"You can pass me the records if you want, sexy," I proposed.

"Come again!"

"Yeah you know, like a caddy," I said.

"Do you honestly think I'm going to stand there all night, passing you records with a broken bloody wrist?"

"No," I answered, "not all night I suppose."

"Not at all you idiot," she clarified.

"Look, let's just get there first," I said, as we raced across the cobbles and onto the High Street.

When we got to the door of *Dibdabs*, the two bouncers stopped us in our tracks and explained that it was a private party tonight. It was actually Jolie who made sense of the situation and spoke first:

"Do you think we'd be here if it wasn't, you Muppet?"

The girl never ceased to impress me. While the doormen were trying their hardest to figure out the correct answer to Jolie's conundrum, Jolie just eyeballed them dauntingly until they submitted and granted us entry; entry to the party we were both invited to anyway.

The one doorman clicked his clicky thing so as to add us to the guest total. I asked him how many were inside, and he informed me that Jolie and I were actually guests number forty-seven and forty-eight, making the party two guests short from becoming a freebie. Surely another two would arrive at some point.

Everyone was there, minus two, plus Lottie. But like the gaffer pointed out – farm animals didn't count. Dave the barman was there, looking reassuringly alive on this occasion. Helping Dave, were Claire and Amy the twins, one of which used to date Marcus a while back, but I could never tell which one (neither could Marcus probably).

Anyway, as Jolie and me waded through the traffic I was a bit put out to spot a couple of Marcus' more senior family members sitting on the black leather sofa.

Who cares if they were old: that was my sofa! They should have been up and dancing to the music with the rest of the well-wishers.

Oh yes, that's a point - the music. Well, to be fair, after being at the party for a few moments, I did come to my senses and accept the fact that Jolie didn't know a single soul, so I deduced that it would be a bit unfair to spend all night behind the wheels of steel. The resident DJ was doing an okay job of things so I decided just to join in with the party instead.

Jolie and me (who by now were even holding hands!) jumped in at the bar, and I asked Claire or Amy (whichever) to look after my record bag and pour a couple of drinks.

Funnily enough, for the third time in a row, it was somehow, once again, my bloody round. As I pulled out my battered wallet to see how close I was to bankruptcy, I suddenly felt the hands of Marcus strike down firmly across my shoulders.

Of course it was Marcus – he was laughing his head off. By that time, he knew exactly what he had done and what I'd been through concerning the sewing pin, and he simply couldn't wait to ridicule me because of it.

Jolie couldn't help herself either. It became quite clear after a just few seconds, that Marcus and Jolie had found some common ground, as they both stood there in stitches at my misfortune.

"Do you want a drink then, dickhead?" I asked Marcus politely.

He just laughed even harder for a while as I stood there waiting for a helpful response. I didn't get one, so I just gave in and smiled as genuinely as possible. At that point Marcus gave me a hug and ordered me to put my wallet away. There was no point in arguing with the lad, and a free drink was going to be about the closest thing to an apology I was going to get.

After the taunting subsided, about five minutes later, I was finally able to properly introduce Jolie to my little brother, when it struck me that Marcus was actually present the evening I first tried (badly) to make my acquaintance with Jolie in the very same bar.

After a brief recap, guess what happened next? That's right – five more minutes of her just mocking me. It was looking to be one of those nights. When I did finally manage to calm the sniggering pair down, I thought it best to prize Jolie away before laughter erupted again, and introduce her to some of my other, less humiliating, family members.

After the barrage of mockery to which I'd been subjected, it gave me great pleasure listening to Jolie have to explain, to practically everyone she met that night, how her wrist happened to be in plaster. However, I think that my family took quite a shine to the girl, and could sense my happiness at being there with her.

By about eleven o'clock a lot of the older guests were starting to leave. There was now a sense that the party was just kicking in and my attention was redirected back towards the music. Jolie seemed happy mingling with other guests, so I plucked up the courage and asked if I could get on the turntables, a request which I was granted.

I retrieved my vinyl from the bar, and, with a bit of help from Marcus, we managed to encourage the DJ to take the rest of the night off. I excitedly took his place and looked over the party-goers.

Now I know I said earlier that I always had an audience when mixing, but it really does make a difference when I can actually see them!

So I rummaged through my bag of filth and pulled out my first record. I put the headphones on and let rip.

Because this was Marcus' leaving party, I wanted to make sure I gave him the blinding set he deserved. Not for this reason alone, I was also eager to impress Jolie with my skills on the decks. Unfortunately for me, however, my alcohol intake, up to that point, was causing other effects than I had intended.

Luckily, everybody else's alcohol consumption meant that nobody really noticed, or even cared about, the complete shambles of a job I was making, and Jolie hardly noticed me playing anyway.

There was another reason why my performance wasn't up to its usual standard. I was getting more and more distracted by the front door!

Guests number forty-nine and fifty were yet to materialize, and the clock was ticking (and tocking). Even though it wasn't my deposit on the line, I just couldn't let the fact rest, that this party needed more guests.

If no more of Marcus' friends or family were due to arrive, then I was just going to have to go out and find some who were.

So that's what I did.

Nobody even noticed that I put one of the bar's CDs on repeat and walked out. My mind was so preoccupied on hitting that half-century that I even forgot to tell Jolie where I was going.

It didn't matter though, because ten minutes after leaving *Dibdabs*, I had returned with a couple of Marcus' 'long lost cousins' who didn't realize that there was a free drink for them at the party.

Looking back now I wish I'd saved my money, considering that when I checked the doorman's counting tool upon our return, it turned out that these two complete random strangers were actually gate-crashers number sixty-six and sixty-seven! Clearly I'd not been paying that much attention to the front door.

Still, it's always better to be safe than sorry in my book: definitely best to invite a couple of strangers to a private party if you're unsure of numbers.

Luckily the rest of the party went without any hiccups and as far as I'm aware, whoever paid the deposit in the first place got their money back.

So, as Dave the barman shut down the music and turned on the main beams to reveal the night's carnage, the majority of well-wishers said their goodbyes to the soon-to-be soldier and left the war zone until just Marcus, Jolie and I remained.

Marcus then turned and spoke out:

"Well my friend, this is it I suppose. We have had some laughs together haven't we? I'm definitely going to miss you and I'll be thinking of you while I'm away. We've been through a lot you and me, and I won't forget about you I promise."

Unfortunately that little heart warmer was for the benefit of the black leather sofa! Marcus even pulled out his mobile phone and took a picture before stroking the thing like the huge cow it once used to be (I promise you, it is bloody comfortable).

My little brother then turned to face me, but before he managed to muster up something sincere, he once again just blurted out in uncontrollable laughter, closely followed by Jolie.

"I'm sorry bruv, but bloody hell, that is some funny shit, come on," was the eventual apology I received from Marcus.

"Yeah hysterical," I sarcastically answered, even though deep down I could relate to the comedy of it all. I'm sure he didn't plan for a sewing-pin to end up in my hip for ten years or so. Who would?

Yeah, so like I expected, I forgave him. The three of us chatted for a while as we waited for our taxis, whilst the twins tidied up the surrounding rubble.

Marcus' cab arrived first. He gave me a final hug, and Jolie a peck on the cheek, and off he went. I watched as the car disappeared around the corner of the High street, leaving Jolie and myself standing on the pavement to say our own goodbyes.

Without attempting to write anything too romantic, I'll just say that basically we exchanged saliva for ten minutes or so until Jolie's cab arrived and that pretty much sealed the deal. She was from that moment on - my fiancée - no sorry - girlfriend. Not the most conventional route to reach that conclusion, but still, we were now officially an item.

You could say that I was over the moon, but, hey diddle diddle, when my taxi arrived forty-five minutes late, I was brought down to earth.

As I finally got my ride home, my mind was working overtime. I was happy to now be with Jolie, but sad that my little brother was leaving. And just to add a big spoonful of confusion into the equation, I was once again totally clueless what my voices were up to.

It's still early days you know. For now I just want my bed.

**CHAPTER 10**

*Way beyond the Point*


It's Monday today: that's good enough. I don't live in Croydon anymore: that's all you need to know. At this precise moment, I'm sitting at a bus stop, playing with my phone. According to the calendar on my phone, it will be Monday in exactly one week's time. I'm not sure what I'll be doing next Monday: I'm not thinking about next Monday for now.

The only thing on my mind at the moment is getting a new phone. In fact, I've been thinking about getting a new phone for weeks now. I've had my head buried in catalogues, papers, and shop windows, tying to decide which phone to buy, and today is the day I am going to buy it.

I am genuinely excited about buying this new phone, and in approximately five minutes or so, the Number Eight will arrive and take me into town so I can make this purchase.

I'm still unsure which phone to buy: there's so many to choose between.

I'm thinking: 'That one you saw in the paper looked quite nice. You'll have to see what they've got when you get into town. I suppose you will be able to sell this phone when you get your new one. I wonder who would like to buy it. It's probably not worth much to be fair. Still, you might get a few quid for it. Oh yeah, there was that advert on the telly: they buy phones. They said that selling your old phone to them is good for the environment. I wonder how selling an old phone is good for the environment. Ha ha, what? Do they bury them, and they grow into trees or something? Good for the environment, my ass. I suppose they need to do everything possible to help this planet though. Mind you, I don't really understand this global warming lark. It doesn't seem to be getting any warmer at all. Last summer was shit: every summer's shit really. I wish it would warm up a bit to be honest. Boy, it was hot when you and Dad went to Crete. Remember the digital thermometer on the end of that clothes rail in the market? It was forty-one degrees, and that was in the shade! Bloody hell! Hey, can you remember that club you went to, and Dad found you on the beach in the morning? That was funny. Oh yeah, isn't there a man-made beach at

Thorpe Park? I'm sure it's at Thorpe Park. Crikey, you haven't been there for donkeys. I can't really remember much about it now: I'm sure there's a beach though. Hey Will, that was a brilliant picture of a beach you made at school using cutouts from magazines. Yeah, you liked art classes. Bit of a bummer getting that American exchange teacher for GCSE though. Only three people passed didn't they? Mr. Richardson wasn't too happy when he got back from America was he. Bloody hell! I'd love to try an American steak though. Someone said it's supposed to taste totally different over there. They're still cows though, aren't they? I wonder what ever happened to mad cow disease? You don't really hear about it anymore do you. You've probably got mad cow disease, Will. Ha ha, moo. Knock knock. Who's there? Cows go. Cows go who? No, cows go moo, not who. Didn't it say on that list of life's instructions at Ben's house, that you should learn at least three clean jokes? What else was on that list? Oh yeah, you should strive for excellence, not perfection. I wonder why that is. I suppose excellence has no limits. Yeah, that's it Will, because if you become perfect, then you can't get any better. Yeah, strive for excellence – good one. What else? Oh yeah, have a firm handshake. Yeah, you've got a firm handshake haven't you? Actually, it really does your head in if someone hasn't got a firm handshake. It's like they don't really want to shake your hand. Ben's got a firm hand shake. Ha ha, he's obviously been reading his list of instructions. I wonder if he returns a car with a full tank of petrol. That was another instruction, wasn't it? No, he doesn't need to borrow cars: he's got his own. He probably would though. Actually, no he wouldn't. Well, he might do I suppose. Are you ever going to learn how to drive Will? No, forget that, you would just end up crashing it: you've already crashed two scooters! That one in Cyprus wasn't even your bloody scooter! I wonder if they noticed all the scratches on the side. Oh forget about it, what sort of bird was that in the harbor, that used to catch the tennis balls? That was crazy! Was it a heron? Was it a flamingo? Lord knows. Anyway, I reckon it's well harsh keeping budgies in cages. Bloody hell, that would do your head in big time, wouldn't it. Oh yeah, I wonder how Tilly's puppies are getting on. They must be big by now. Hey, can you remember Scrabble the boxer? That was a class dog. I wonder who came up with the name – Scrabble? Dad probably… D - O - G - G - Y, three-hundred points, triple word score, thank you very much, now show me the money. Come on - show me - don't be scared…What the hell are you going on about Will? Behave yourself please. Scared, scared, you're not scared are you Will? Nobody's scared, everybody's rosy. Hey, remember when you were a kid and you went through a carwash for the first time? That was scary! Ha ha, you plonker, what's so scary about that? Oh sugar, is that the bus coming? Yes, no, yes, no, yes, no, yes, yes, yes it is. Hooray! Three cheers for the bus: hip, hip, hip, hop, hip hop, hippos hopping, hopping, hopping, everywhere. Come on Will, sort it out mate. I hope you've got enough change: let's have a look. That's a point, how much is the bus nowadays? It keeps going up…Yeah, that should be enough Will, rock and roll baby, yeah! Oh hang on a minute - where the hell are you going? Umm…Think Will, think, think, think, quick, quick, quick… Too late…'

"Single to town please."

"Ninety-five."

"Thanks a lot."

'Sugar, sugar, sugar, sugar, sugar, where the hell were you going Will?Market? No. Music shop? No. You're not meeting anyone are you? No. Any appointments? Doubt it. Oh just sit down and chill out: it will come to you. Here, he looks a bit strange, sit at the back so he can't see you. Lovely… I wonder who gets paid more, bus drivers or taxi drivers. You couldn't be a bus driver Will: I doubt they would let you. Actually, I wonder if you are allowed to drive buses. No, forget that, you would just end up killing everyone. I hope they didn't notice all the scratches on the side of that scooter. No, it wasn't too bad was it? Not as bad as your knee anyway. I don't think you've got any scars, have you? Oh yeah, there's that little one on your finger when you tried slicing a baguette with a razor-blade. That was clever, wasn't it? Oh your phone's ringing… Oh it's only Mum.'

"Hi Mum."

"Hello love: you all right?"

"Yeah, fine ta."

"Did you get it?"

"Get what?"

"Your phone."

"What phone?"

"Your new phone."

"New phone, new phone, new phone, oh yeah, that's what I'm doing now."

"What, did you forget?"

"No, of course not."

"I see. Well, I was just phoning to check you were okay."

"Yeah, fine ta."

"Where are you?"

"On the bus into town."

"Okay, so long as you're okay."

"Yeah, fine ta."

"Good, well give us a ring with your new phone when you get it, if you want."

"Will do Mum."

"Okay, see you."

"Yep, see you Mum."

"Cheerio then."

"Bye."

It's Monday today, and the only thing on my mind at the moment, is getting a new phone.

# CHAPTER 11

## The Bare Essentials: Extras Not Included

I won't lie to you: I'm trying to get this book published. If you know anyone who could help – please let me know. Then again, if you're reading this, the chances are that your help is no longer required. Oh well – thanks anyway.

In all honesty, that wasn't the reason why this work started in the first place: my initial intention was to write a book for my dad's birthday present. Considering how fond of books he is, I figured that a specimen from his own son would be a great idea. However, as soon as I started writing, I decided that I had some serious points to make, which needed projecting to a wider audience. Wasn't really sure what points exactly, but concluded that there must be something relevant floating around, deep within the psychedelic contents of my muddled skull. So off I went – freestyle. And here we are now.

Anyway, if by some sort of freak accident – someone (preferably an individual who's crazier than I am, who's also a compulsive gambler, with vast quantities of money to burn) decides to publish this book, I can just give Dad the original manuscript. Who knows? – Could be priceless one day (no harm in wishful thinking you know). In fact – sod it – I'll go the extra mile and even sign it for him (like I mentioned earlier – it's nice to be nice).

Dad had been playing a key role in the production of this work, up until recently. At least twice a week, I would show my face at the bookstall to refer to his second-hand, jumbo-sized dictionary. Unknown to me, however, this regular occurrence was becoming an irritation for Dad, to say the least. That was until the day I turned up with my little (yet very important) list of words – only to find that he'd sold the damned thing. He most certainly saw the funny side concerning that little sale, as he cackled uncontrollably after breaking me the hilarious bad news.

Regardless of his cruelty, I discovered that my dear old dad does, in fact, have a heart, when two days later, he presented me with my very own, brand, spanking-new, 'Book of Spells' – one far superior to the previous one I'd referred to.

This one came with its own thesaurus built-in as standard – fantastic! I never even realised that there was such a thing! This magical invention gives you the freedom to choose from a variety of words with the same meaning, rearrange them to suit your own personal preference, and create multiple sentences that all suggest the same bloody thing!

I was so thrilled to own such a useful piece of kit, I was unfazed to learn that Dad had purchased it for just quarter the original price at some 'bargain book bonanza'. He probably sensed the disappointment on my face, so felt a bit guilty when he sold his dictionary at the stall, leaving me to go home without whatever vital information I needed regarding one word or another.

Dad might have thought it was funny, because a dictionary is probably the last book he would ever need to read. After years and years of reading book after book, Dad was actually turning into one, big, tubby, walkin', talkin', human dictionary, with all the knowledge of the English language that he would ever need. The man is like a machine when it comes to reading: it's a wonder how I'd come so far in life without reading a single book myself, really. Obviously something I didn't inherit from my dad, along with his monster beer-gut and shiny bald patch. There's still time I suppose!

Not a prob now, cheers – Bob. Following the time I initially embarked on this unfamiliar literary mission, my vocabulary has indubitably proven to be immeasurably enlarged and refined compared to any prior, and conceivably primitive, apprehension I once held towards this: our own personal and ever-flourishing, complex yet unquestionably gracious, language, recognised by such a profound and significantly grandiose percentage of our planet's total population – as *La Langue Anglaise*. (I think that's French.)

Not only this though, I'm proud to say that somewhere in the middle of the third chapter, I managed to move away from using the type-with-one-finger-technique and began coordinating two fingers (together), and by chapter five, I have to say, I was getting pretty damned good.

*The words are flowing with such harmonious grace now, that I might be finished by tonight – that's if I can continue writing only of important matters, such as, everything so far, leading up to this critical point in time.*

Right then – what was I talking about? Ah yes, Dad and his priceless input to this work. I've got to be honest with you: it's the books he's got that have been the real help. The book about palmistry was the exception: I would probably have made more sense out of that one if I had no hands!

On the other hand, I did pick up a book about publishing that I've briefly flicked through. In the section concerning what a publisher wants, or more importantly what a publisher doesn't want, I learned that a lot of people who write autobiographies (not that this book – strictly speaking – is one), like to include a chapter about their experiences of moving house.

I imagine that, to a publisher, this could potentially get annoyingly repetitive if faced with such stories on a regular basis. But I can also see why it's a popular topic to discuss due to the fact that 'moving day' tends to be packed with drama that could be worthy of disclosure. I started thinking.

After some careful consideration over the next couple of days, I finally decided – at the risk of sounding ordinary – to reveal my own experiences of 'moving day' – regardless of the potential damage this could cause. In any case, that's what this whole chapter will be based on.  But I'll meet you half way and only incorporate the bare essentials – deal? I don't want to waste your time more than necessary with a load of nonsense – so I won't.

Okay, here we go then, from the top –

## CHAPTER 11(REDUX)

### *The Bare Essentials: Extras Not Included*

March 2, 2006: Judgement Day.

The day I moved into my present abode, accompanied by my fiancée – no sorry – girlfriend, and her little boy.

It was to be the umpteenth occasion I would flee from Mum's part-time nest, since the first time I'd tried it at the naive age of sixteen. Thereafter, I began to display boomerang-like characteristics. Until the time I actually moved as far away as Croydon – I had foiled my every previous attempt at independence, by nipping back to Mum's for a nice hot bath, and a mug of hot-chocolate.

I think we were both quietly confident, that the move to Croydon was to be my last from home, but because things were still unsettled, allowances were made for my return.

Nevertheless, on this, my most recent, departure, when Mum gently locked her fingers around my arm and uttered the words, 'I love you, William, but enough is enough now, okay.' I knew she meant business. My suspicions proved true, and soon it was clear that she didn't want me back under any circumstances whatsoever!

Do you know what she went and did? I'll tell you what. Literally two weeks after me and all my worldly possessions were safely gone, and the keys were back in her custody, she only went and put her own house on the market, with seemingly freakish plans of downsizing to a smaller one. She made out that it was because Eric couldn't cope with the garden anymore – but I suspected ulterior motives.

Regardless of what I might have suspected, I wasn't too bothered, and besides, she didn't need reasons. Maybe she just wanted to enjoy a peaceful retirement with her husband: a plan that didn't happen include a man in his mid-twenties, (who's quite partial to a bit of loud dance-music from time to time), eating all the chocolate biscuits and drinking all the beers. You can't really blame them: I'm not sure if I could live with 'Me' either. It's comforting in a way, knowing that I don't have a choice in the matter.

In saying this though – Me is a decent enough bloke to be fair. He can get a bit uptight, now and again, but generally he's quite a fun person to be around. He's so paranoid though. Sometimes he gets these ideas into his head that people are watching him: planning to hurt him – including his family and friends! I try to tell him that he's being silly, and I know he wants to believe it's all rubbish, but he just can't seem to snap out of his irrational way of thinking. 'Me' makes out to people that everything's fine, but I know that sometimes he's not as fine as he lets on.

Mum has had a hard time understanding 'Me' since his return from Croydon, but what's been happening to him is a pretty tough thing to understand anyway. I mean, Me's still trying to figure it out for himself, and, hopefully (with a bit of luck), one day – he will and I am going to help in anyway possible.

It turned out that despite Mum's determination to make sure this move was a one-way ticket only, she clearly didn't intend to banish me from her life totally. Shortly after the sale of her house, Mum and Eric just so happened to move into a nice little Georgian terraced house, just a convenient stone's throw away from ours. I see her more than ever these days.

Maybe Eric really was struggling with the garden after all. I suppose he is nearly seventy. Oh, okay – I'm feeling a bit guilty now. I don't think I offered to mow the lawn once. Come to think of it, I really should have helped out more with a lot of jobs around the house. I know for a fact that such idleness wouldn't wash with Jolie. When she asks me to do something, I tell her, 'yes I can do that for you right now babe.' An alternative answer would just be hazardous for my health, which has already apparently deteriorated mentally.

Anyway, I'm starting to get sidetracked. Enough of the chitchat: I'm supposed to be telling you all about my move.

Okay, let me think back for a minute. It was March 2, 2006: I know that much. There's not a lot else to say really – considering I'm only going to stick to the bare essentials. For any of you who have experienced your own 'moving day' – the rest will sound relatively familiar I'm sure.

There was a lot of boxes and newspaper floating about the place; lots of lifting heavy things up the stairs. There was the worry that furniture wouldn't fit through the door, along with communication such as, 'don't drop that – it's fragile,' and, 'left a bit – no too much – right a bit,' and, 'is the hot coming through yet?' and, 'shall we just get a Chinese tonight?' – you know, the usual. Yes there was drama, but if you really want to know about how I had to knock on the neighbour's door and ask him to move his car, then you'll have to give me a ring and I'll tell you all about it.

I can see now why publishers get tired of hearing about moving house! To be fair, I don't really look back on any of my experiences of moving house with excitement, so realistically, why would I enjoy reading about someone else's?

All you need to know is that we lived apart and now we don't. From that pivotal day forth – we have shared each other's company, in our current house that I told you about earlier: the weird one with the three storeys.

That's right, we are still there to this present day. It's such a heavy house you know. I mean I haven't tried lifting it up or anything, but the damned thing is definitely subsiding. You can tell because the great view from the top floor I mentioned, is slowly getting worse and worse (don't suppose the neighbour's extension project is helping matters either).

A tilting house does make life easier when cleaning up Matty's marbles though – they end up congregating in the corner of his bedroom; saving both time, and broken ankles.

So now you know where I live: just look out for the leaning tower of Shrewsbury. Get the picture? Okay good, now let's move swiftly on.

What next then people?

Chapter 12 sounds like just the ticket.

## CHAPTER 12

## Just the Ticket

March 2, 2006: moved in with Jolie.

November 14, 2006: had over nine months of living with the love of my life and her little boy, to realise just how much family life can drill your brain!

Talk about arguments! Mind you, even now, arguing with Jolie is always pointless, due to her frighteningly sharp tongue, with its whole string of vile language, that would frighten anyone who's brave (and stupid) enough to stand up to her. I'm not saying that she's never had good reason to get mad at me, but even if I've got a good point to make in one of our conflicts, she always makes my point sound totally irrelevant, and continues targeting me with her 1000v audio drill.

It doesn't help that no matter who's right or wrong, little Matty always ends up taking his mother's side, leaving me with nowhere to turn except for the front door: a defensive move that gets me into more trouble than anything else.

Nine months! Looking back now, it hasn't been too bad, I suppose. Despite the fighting, and Matty's occasional behavioural problems, there have been a lot of good times too.

Regarding my mental health concerns, Jolie had always been great: meaning, she always found the patience to listen to my issues with an open mind. Whether she ever believed any of my theories remained unclear, and yet her support always appeared to be genuine.

Having someone who accepted these matters was important to me, and a rare comfort to find. I struggle to think of too many people in my life now, who truly accept me for being me. Instead, people seem to put on this friendly front, which is about as clear as bullshit and deeply patronising.

Nine months, hey. Yeah, Mum was happy too by then. Despite moving into a smaller house with her husband Eric, making my return virtually impossible in the event of a catastrophe, my own progress was apparent to her, and so was the bond between the two families. By progress, I mean I was doing okay. I was walking a few dogs to get me out the house for a bit: that was until someone informed me that some insurance might be a good idea in the running of such a business. I failed to see the harm: the two German Shepherds just seemed to like biting each other to pieces, and left everyone else alone.

I've always liked dogs: the main reason being that I trust them: no chance that a dog could have any involvement in a plot to destroy my world. Yeah, dogs are loyal like that you know: dogs and babies – both harmless in my book.

Yeah nine months – you could say that I'd found some kind of direction in my life again, which never seemed likely since the Croydon days, but now things were really starting to blossom.

November 14, 2006: Jolie's belly was really ballooning by this date too! In fact, our little baby's arrival was a week overdue, showing few signs of materialising. We had both accepted that we would be meeting the new addition in about a week's time: the day when the midwife would have to pull her out using all necessary force available.

It was exciting times for all of us – including little Matty. He was getting impatient, and just wanted mummy to hurry up and squeeze his little sister out (it's frightening what kids pick up on these days). I think he was getting sick of talking to Jolie's belly, and found the whole thing a bit stupid.

"She will come out when she's ready," Jolie would explain to him, "she just needs a bit more time to prepare herself that's all."

I wasn't really surprised she was running a bit late. As things at home were blossoming – so was Jolie's temper. Over the previous few months, arguments escalated, and Matty'sbehaviour had become horrendous. I used every argument as a ticket to go up town on the razz, just so I could breathe some peaceful air. No wonder the baby was happy staying put!

I had been looking for an opportunity to re-propose before the birth of our child, but it was looking unlikely, to say the least. I was, however, better prepared this time: my heart-warming speech was firmly rehearsed inside my head, making me feel that rejection was unlikely. My confidence of success, this time, was boosted by events the previous week.

Unknown to Jolie, I had received a phone call from Shrewsbury's bus depot. At first I thought the woman on the other end of the line had lost her marbles, but it turned out that she was actually phoning to say that nobody ended up claiming the package I'd found on the bus, and so it was there waiting for me to collect.

This was of great benefit to me, considering that one of the items was a pretty gold ring, one highly superior to the previous silver number I'd had an enthusiastic friend make for me for forty quid. It was supposed to be thirty, but he decided to incorporate a small stone as a centre-piece: a stone that wouldn't have looked out of place in the bottom of someone's fish tank!

The designer coat was taken to a charity shop to avoid any unnecessary questioning by Jolie (she wouldn't have liked it anyway), leaving me free to produce the ring at the time of reckoning, with little to worry about how I got it. All I needed now was a good time: a good time was looking bleak, and November 14, 2006 was looking impossible, due to the morning's argument over the state of the clean dishes.

I was on the piss. I had been on this particular piss all day and I truly was pissed – very pissed! By ten o'clock I was steaming; desperately needing to replace this lost piss with food, before going home for a night of shit.

I stumbled through the streets, trying to decide what to eat, avoiding the local pizza joint like the plague, and ending up, instead, in the Turkish kebab house just down the road from ours – the one with the reputation for serving up crap.

Falling down the only step to fall down, and smashing into the counter – confirmed the Turk's fears, that someone who was very, very drunk had just entered their establishment. They paid me no attention, as I was holding onto the counter to support myself, whilst vainly trying to focus on the menu. This behaviour was probably a regular occurrence in such kebab houses, and clearly ignored. The Turks just continued yapping in the back room and laughing at their own jokes. I might have laughed too, but I didn't understand a single word they were saying, so instead, I just got more and more vexed with the lack of service. Even my banging and shouting received zero attention, and my hunger only enhanced my anger.

After about five minutes of posing like a lemon, I decided that the only way I was going to get fed, was to serve myself.

So that's what happened. I walked around the counter and grabbed myself three king-size chicken skewers, fresh off the tray, and a handful of sweet corn to take out – and all of this without anyone in the back room lifting a finger! In fact the only time they acknowledged me was when I shouted 'thanks a lot,' on my way out the door. My custom was clearly very much appreciated. And so it should be! I got outside and realised that I was going to have to cook these particular kebabs myself!

So next I wobbled up the hill towards our house, waving these bloody kebabs in the air like the Olympic torch. You could tell which way I walked by the trail of sweet corn, all the way up the wrong side of the main road. It would be fair to say – I was in a mess!

Things were about to get messier. I was heading into certain hell, and all I had to say in my defence was that I'd brought the dinner home: raw – stolen – kebabs. Fantastic! There wasn't even any sweet corn left to go with them. In fact, if the Turks noticed that their kebabs had gone walkies, the jolly green giant would have lead them right up to my front door!

Regardless of my stupidity, and after a brief period of reflection by the front gate, it seemed clear that the situation was repairable, and there really was nothing to worry about. Like a big brave boy, I reached for my keys and stepped into the house.

The screaming and groaning was coming from upstairs, so I knew Jolie was home. Her sister, Sally, had also turned up, because I could hear her telling Jolie that everything was going to be all right, and just to take deep breaths. At the time, all I could think was that I must have really pissed her off this time. To me, I'd done the dishes cleanly enough by any normal person's standard, so she was the one in the wrong – not me. Still, I cautiously tiptoed up the stairs and onto the landing. They were in the kitchen – oblivious to my presence. I poked my head up the second flight of stairs to see that all the lights were off – indicating that Matty wasn't home. No option, but to walk through the kitchen door and face the music. Unfortunately, this particular 'music' was foreign to me, and I really didn't have a clue how to dance to it. Instead I just lunged through, waving three raw kebabs in the air, hoping that everything was fine. It wasn't.

"Hi Jools, you okay baby?" I spluttered, followed by, "Sal, what a pleasant surprise."

"Where the fuck have you been you little shit?" Jolie retorted. She was down on all fours, her sister dampening her head with a wet flannel.

"Is everything okay baby?" I asked. "You don't look too well."

"Is everything okay? Is everything okay? No, Will, everything's not fucking okay, you tosser," she sneered.

"Why, what's the matter?" I asked.

"Isn't it obvious you prick?" she screamed. "I'm having your bloody baby, you stupid idiot!"

"What – right now? I've just brought dinner home love," followed by, "here Sal, there's a kebab for you too if you want one."

"Will, are you off your head mate?" said Sally. "Your woman is about to give birth, and you're thinking about dinner. Are you bloody stupid or what?"

"Seriously you two, these kebabs will take literally…"

"JUST BOOK ME A FUCKING TAXI NOW BEFORE I STICK THOSE KEABS RIGHT UP YOUR FUCKING ASSHOLE!" shouted Jolie.

"Okay, okay, I'm on it, I'm on it: to the hospital, yeah?" I asked.

"Yes, Will, that's right – to the hospital," Sally confirmed.

I put the kebabs on the side and rummaged through my pockets.

"I can't find my phone, babe," I said.

"How fucking convenient!" said Jolie sarcastically.

"Seriously, baby, I must have left it in the pub or something, because it's definitely not in my pockets."

I continued to search my empty pockets for the phone that I definitely knew wasn't there, in the vain hope that one would magically materialise, and save me from my predicament.

"WILL ONE OF YOU JUST RING ME A TAXI BEFORE I GIVE BIRTH RIGHT HERE ON THE FUCKING KITCHEN FLOOR!"

"Here, Will, just use mine, mate," Sally interrupted. "You just keep breathing, sis — you're doing great."

"Yeah, just breathe baby, that's brilliant," I said, and took the phone.

Twenty minutes later and the taxi arrived. I had sobered up in record time, and was now on the ball, so much so, that I even remembered to run upstairs and grab the new and improved engagement ring. Time was running out.

After a brief discussion between the two sisters, it was decided that I was in a fit enough state to handle the situation, and take Jolie to the Royal Shrewsbury myself. The taxi driver got us there in record time too! I think the geezer was a bit concerned about the possible flood that his car's interior was threatened by, so he ignored the Highway Code and all its speed cameras. As it happened, the only water to break was the sweat dripping from my forehead.

We got out of the taxi, and I gave Flash Gordon a considerable tip for his sense of urgency — probably not enough to cover the speeding fines, but adequate to buy the man a bottle of vodka to calm his nerves. I grabbed a wheelchair from the lobby, and bolted Jolie down the maternity ward corridors – trying to find someone to pull our baby out.

Due to Jolie's cunning but utterly fake 'latex allergy', we ended up in a five-star delivery room with all mod cons – away from the standard-class riffraff. Still, there was no time for luxuries, and as soon as Jolie was lying on the bed, the midwife was ordering her to push.

The next few hours were deeply emotional. As soon as the midwife told me to come down to her end of the bed, I could see the top of the baby's head, with a thick layer of dark hair slightly protruding from the inside of Jolie's vagina. It was at this precise moment that I remembered the ring. Through the shouting and the screaming (which was far too graphic to describe), I stood again at Jolie's side, pulled out the little golden gem, rehearsed my speech in my head – and let rip:

"Baby – you're gorgeous – I love you – will you marry me please?"

"YOU WHAT?" was the answer.

"Marry me?" I repeated.

"WHAT?"

"Marry me?"

"ARE YOU FUCKING SERIOUS?" she shouted, "YOU'RE HONESTLY ASKING ME TO MARRY YOU WHEN I'VE GOT HALF A BABY STICKING OUT OF ME YOU KNOB?"

"Well, will you or not, babe?"

"Can you two shut up please?" requested the midwife, "Jolie, can you just concentrate on pushing – she's almost here."

"I'M GOING TO FUCKING EAT YOU WILL: AAAAAAAAAAAAAAAAAAAAAAAAAGGGGGGGGGGGH!"

'Please don't be a lady-boy, please don't be a lady-boy', I thought: my fingers tightly crossed.

Pop – and there she was – our little baby. 11.30pm, November 14, 2006 and my knees never felt so weak. I nearly collapsed – she was beautiful and I was speechless. It was without a doubt the most amazing experience I've ever had. That was until I saw the midwife pulling out the placenta! Still, my Jolie had done it: she'd given me the gift of my first child, who happened to be born on the same day as the Prince of Wales (could be a sign of some sort).

As I stood there gazing at our precious baby, happily sharing a moment of peacefulness with my fiancée – no sorry – girlfriend, all Jolie could say was:

"Let me have a look at that ring again."

I thought my luck was in, until I saw her face. Her bemused expression gave me the horrible indication, that the previous hoo-hah which I thought was going to subside was doing no such thing – but I didn't know why…

Now I know what you're thinking. What the hell does this chapter have to do with a ticket? To be honest – I haven't got a bloody clue! There's no deeper meaning so don't think too hard: I know I'm not the ticket – that's for sure! We didn't even get to the hospital by train so that won't wash. I'm sure my daughter wouldn't like to grow up and find out I referred to her as a ticket either – so what's left?

Poetic justice, I guess.


**An Anecdote regarding Jolie**

September 28, 2004: I remember the day well.

It was the day Marcus and myself met in *Dibdabs* and got extremely drunk: the day when I ate a slice of pizza hotter than the sun: the day it rained enough to sort out the world's drought problems. It was the day that I noticed Jolie for the first time, as I sat on a bus, on my way into town.

Well at the time, I wasn't sure if September 28, 2004 was a good day for me or not, but for Jolie – it most certainly wasn't!

As she sat at the bar in *Dibdabs*, dripping with rain and sucking on her drink, there was a very good reason why her face looked like thunder. I didn't know why at the time: all I could do was sit back on the black leather sofa next to Marcus, completely mesmerised by everything about her. She was an angel – an absolute angel: a pissed off angel by the look of it, and I'll tell you exactly why.

I never realised it until later, but the old man who lived at the back of mum's old house, was actually Jolie's grandfather. His name's Arthur and he still lives there now. He owns a little white terrier, which I've regularly seen him take for walks around the estate, when I used to live at mum's. This vicious little canine would often escape from his back garden into ours through a small hole in the hedge, every chance he got. He was a bloody menace to say the least.

Arthur used to live with his late wife, Hannah (Jolie's grandmother), who, unfortunately, died from a heart attack in August of that year. She had been unwell for some time, so the news of her death came as no surprise to us really.

I didn't really know Hannah too well, just her name. The only time I used to see her was if I was returning their dog after one of its prison breaks. It seemed that no matter how much you tried to fill the gaps in the hedge, the little mutt would still manage to find a way through.

Hannah was a sweet lady. Let's see – she must have been in her early eighties when she died. She always seemed to take forever to answer the door to me, but she regularly offered me money or biscuits, for safely returning the dog, rewards which I would always refuse.

One day when I went round with the pooch, she requested that I come in to change a light-bulb because Arthur was out somewhere – so I obliged. I vaguely remember us talking about her granddaughters; I can't remember everything she said, but the girls were all spoken of very highly indeed – although she did secretly have a favourite.

Even though I didn't know Jolie or her sisters when I was living back at my mum's old place, I can say that they have always spoken very highly of their grandmother too. As well as this, Jolie and myself have been to visit Arthur on a couple of occasions since Hannah's death. The identity of her new boyfriend came as a surprise to him: me being the lad next door who used to rescue his dog and play all that horrible music.

"Oh my beautiful granddaughter has come to see me," he would welcome us. "And she's brought her noisy neighbour boyfriend too."

Luckily he did have a sense of humour, so there were no bad feelings really. Nevertheless, I'm sure that he has not missed my loud dance music since I moved away. Anyway, the bad feelings that might have been present were soon forgotten when Jolie informed him of a good deed I once did: a deed I was unaware I'd made at all, unaware until the birthday of our child.

September 28, 2004: the day started out brightly.

Hannah's funeral had taken place just a few weeks previously, and Arthur had invited Jolie round to discuss something of great importance. Jolie was still having driving-lessons back then and was yet to pass her test, so she visited her Grandfather on the morning of the 28th – by bus.

The sun was shining that morning, but the forecast indicated (correctly) that it could change to rain by the afternoon. It was for this reason, that Jolie packed her favourite coat in a plastic bag before setting off that day. She must have had her hands full too. Not only was Jolie visiting her grandfather, but Matty was also visiting his great-grandfather, making getting about just that little bit more stressful.

Now I said that Hannah secretly had a favourite grandchild. It was Hannah who paid for the driving lessons, so I don't think I need to tell you which grandchild it was. It turned out that Hannah's last wish was that the wedding-ring given to her by Arthur over forty years ago should be handed down into the safe hands of her very much loved granddaughter – Jolie.

Now Jolie might have been loved more than anything, but one thing's for sure – her hands weren't that safe! Two hours after the deeply emotional hand-over of this ring, Jolie went and left the bloody thing on a bus – in a plastic bag – with a designer coat! She was devastated! More importantly, she didn't have a clue where it could be! Even after retracing her steps in the pouring rain all afternoon, she simply never thought about checking 'lost property': the place where I took the bag after finding it on the same damned bus.

Who would have thought it? I bet she never imagined that I'd be proposing to her with her grandmother's ring at the birth of our child. She just accepted that the ring was lost. None of her other family knew about the misplaced inheritance, so she just kept the whole incident a secret.

When I did propose in the hospital, I couldn't figure out whether to laugh or cry! I ended up crying, though, when I discovered that the coat I gave to a charity-shop actually cost three hundred quid!

Jolie wasn't bothered about the coat: she had her grandmother's ring back, and yet she still said 'No' to my proposal! How unfair is that? After everything I said about how it's nice to be nice too! What else would it take? How was I to win her hand in marriage?

"Why won't you just say yes, damn it!"

Hannah must be looking down upon us and laughing her head off.

**Holy Jolie**


So what can I say about Jolie that you don't already know? You know that we live together in a three-storey house in Shrewsbury. You know that we also share this house with her son Matty, and now you know that Matty's got a new little playmate, in the form of our daughter – Sarah.

Oh wait a second – no – you didn't know that did you? That's right, we decided three weeks after our beautiful daughter was born that we should, in fact, give her a name. The plan to choose her a name when she was born never materialised, and so much time had now elapsed that even our family members were getting tired of calling her 'little baby.' We were left with no choice – we had to name her something!

So we named her Sarah. I wanted to call her Billie. It was my given (but then taken) right to call her Billie, too. Before we found out what sex our baby was going to be, we agreed that if a little boy popped out, then Jolie could name him; if a little girl, then the honour was mine. The honour was only mine, however, as long as what I chose was what Jolie wanted. My choice of the name 'Billie' was out of the question, even before it was mentioned. So much for our so-called 'deal'! Sarah remained nameless for three whole weeks because Jolie disliked every name I came up with, after, and including, Billie. Eventually, I had to pretend that Sarah was the name I'd really wanted to call her all along, and agree that 'Billie' was totally ridiculous!

"You can't call her that, you idiot!" she would explode. "All the school kids will be calling her 'Silly Billie' in the playground."

In the end, I had to agree that she was right, so we eventually decided on 'Sarah'. It's still a nice name though, and, to be honest, I'm glad we did have a girl, because if she would've been a he – Jolie was stuck on Derry! What would all the school kids be saying then?

Still, it's nice for Matty to have someone else to focus his attention towards. I wouldn't say he isn't naughty anymore, but his improvement must be noted, and the future's looking bright.

Right then, enough about that: what else do you need to know about Jolie? I gather it's clicked that her language can leave a lot to be desired. I've never met anyone who swears so many times in one sentence! One morning, I purposely counted how many times she used the 'f' word before lunchtime, only to lose count after the first few hundred, within an hour of her waking up!

Her sisters are just as bad! Ah that's a point – her sisters. I haven't really said much about her sisters. Well there are two of them – Sally (who I have mentioned), and Stacey.

Jolie is the oldest of the three, being just a couple of years older than me. Then there's Sally in the middle, with Stacey, aged twenty-one, being the youngest.

Now believe me when I say this: they – are – all – completely – bonkers! I must have had a death wish when getting together with Jolie, because it has been like taking on the whole family – which is great, so long as there are no problems between Jolie and myself. An argument with my girlfriend can rapidly erupt into a family onslaught, even when my girlfriend is quite capable of doing the job herself! I'm telling you – these girls are dangerous: oozing with attitude and not afraid to use it. They operate like the power-rangers; meaning that, if there's a problem too big for one sister to deal with, the girls instead combine forces, to create an all powerful, horrid but indestructible force, capable of sending the problem packing with its tail quivering between its legs. I'm not joking – even Charlie couldn't control these angels!

Their own mum's not frightened of getting her hands dirty either! Between the four of them, you would need a small army, and balls of steel, to stand any chance of getting your voice heard at all! Still, they do have a nice side too. I haven't seen much evidence of this so far, but people have told me it's true. It must be nice however, to belong to such a tight family unit, where you do feel brave enough to take on the world, regardless of having any just cause to do so or not!

Despite my own personal arguments with the girls, they have helped me out in times of need – so for that I'm grateful (I think).

Their mum (Carol) owns a small chocolate shop in town called *Cacao Loco*, where all three sisters work together (fitting name come to think of it). The chocolates are all hand-made by the girls, and have become famous in Shrewsbury, purely for their exceptional quality and eccentric flavours. The business thrives, and probably would thrive more, if half the town wasn't too frightened to shop there.

Jolie told me a story once, about how Stacey and she were working together at the shop, and this teenage girl walked in eating a bag of truffles purchased from one rival's outlet or another. Apparently, after the brave shopper received a full-blown telling off by Stacey, the youngest sister then proceeded to grab the poor girl's truffles from the palm of her hands. She then, literally, kicked her out of the shop, launched the truffles one by one straight back at her (abuse included), as the petrified girl darted up the street trying to avoid her own flying delicacies.

I wasn't surprised in the slightest. I'm fully aware of what they're capable of: to the extent that I've had to get a friend to go into the shop for me, when requiring a box of their superb chilli and white-chocolate truffles for Mother's day. I've even walked the long way through town, just to avoid walking past the window!

Still, Jolie is my sweetheart and I can't help but love her. She always tells me how much she loves me too:

"More than you'll ever know," she says.

To which I reply:

"More than I'll ever understand you mean, baby."

She goes from one extreme to another: permanently running hot and cold, making it extremely difficult to know what the hell she wants. We could have a heated argument over apparently nothing, when it turns out that I didn't give her a kiss when leaving the house to get the milk in the morning. Now this could be understandable, if she hadn't practically kicked me out of the house to get the milk that morning, during a whole separate argument. I'm permanently confused! Nevertheless, she loves me to bits (more than I'll ever understand).

So what else can I say about her. Well, let me think for a minute…

Well, she's one in a million. To be frank, she's more like one in a zillion. I've never met another girl who can make your heart melt with her smile, and, within the same breath, make you crap your trousers! Unpredictable just doesn't quite cover it, somehow. She certainly keeps me guessing, that's for sure. I'm not sure if it's a good thing for my fragile head really, not being able to relax, but honestly I've always enjoyed a bit of excitement in my life, keeps things fresh.

And that's it, I suppose, nothing else to say about her, except...

Oh... She's, funny – kind – ambitious – gorgeous – scary – naughty – understanding – open-minded – caring – enthusiastic – realistic – honest – thoughtful – organised – intelligent, oh yeah – and downright sexy! All the things a man could wish for really, with a few added extras.

Boy, I'm lucky!

## CHAPTER 13

### Got to Get Down to Move Up!

January 4, 2007:it was all Jolie's idea – not mine. I thought I'd never see the day. Any previous thoughts I had about tackling January 4, 2007 were soon discarded, due to the fact that this specific day was simply too frightening to really contemplate.

But Jolie insisted that January 4, 2007 was in fact a great idea: the perfect way to start the New Year. I couldn't see it. Fair enough, my resolution list was already looking bleak, but this was just suicide!

Nevertheless, January 4, 2007 happened: a reality I thought I'd never experience. A reality I never wanted to experience either, but Jolie had to know best, and went and booked the train ticket anyway.

"Where's yours then, baby?" I wondered aloud, as she'd presented me with my own orange ticket, some days earlier.

"What do you mean mine?" she replied. "You're going on your own."

"What do you mean 'on my own'?" I panicked.

"Well I can't come with you," she said. "I've got to look after the kids."

"They can come too," I offered.

"No Will," she countered. "This is something you should do on your own baby."

"But I haven't been back to Croydon since everything went wrong babe."

"Exactly," she stated, "this could be really helpful for you."

"Helpful? I'm going to shit myself!"

"Oh don't be so stupid Will," argued Jolie. "You'll be fine – trust me."

"Trust you? Are you serious?"

"What's that supposed to mean?" she asked. "Anyway, I've booked your ticket now, so tough."

"Well I don't know what to say sweetie."

"How about a 'Thank you', William?"

"Yeah, nice one – really appreciate it."

"You will."

"Will I?"

"Darling, stop being such a wimp."

"Baby, those people told me to get out of Croydon."

"Yes, but if they were warning you about the flat collapsing, then it will be safe to go back now won't it?" she quizzed me, tolerantly.

Baby that's just one theory, okay," I argued. "They might still want to kill me!"

"Why would anyone want to kill you?"

"I don't know baby," I answered. "Maybe they just don't like me."

"Stop being a wimp," she insisted. "You're getting on that train."

"I'm not up for it babe."

"Tough."

"I won't go."

"You are going!"

"I'm not!"

"You are!"

"No!"

"WILL!"

January 3, 2007: and my nerves were shot. I'd bitten my fingernails so much that I didn't have any nails anymore – just fingers.

That evening I paced around the house like a malfunctioning robot, trying to find someway to settle down, but couldn't. Unfortunately for me, January 4, 2007 was looming ever closer.

"Will, come to bed," pleaded Jolie. "You're making me dizzy."

"Wait a second," I replied. "I'm just taking time to think."

"You know, thinking isn't a good idea, sweetie," she replied. "Just come to bed and relax."

"I am relaxed, okay."

"Oh yeah, of course you are Will. That's why tonight you've done fifteen miles between here and the kitchen!"

"I'm just preparing myself, baby."

"Will, you're going to Croydon on a train, not running a marathon."

"I know that," I said, "but people are going to know I'm coming and I have to expect the worst."

"I understand," she replied, "but it will be fine, I promise."

"Well I hope you're right, that's all I can say."

I got undressed, and climbed under the duvet.

"Will, the baby's crying."

"Great stuff!"

Well, January 4, 2007 began at midnight, but it really only got under way for me at 7.00am, when the alarm clock rudely awoke me from my dream, just as I was about to save Shrewsbury from the deadly dragon-robot, with its enormous, laser-firing fangs. Another ten minutes sleep, and you just know I would have done it.

Anyway, despite my trepidation the previous night about the next day's onslaught, I felt quite positive as I rose from my bed. I did the usual morning thing. You know: shower, teeth, breakfast, coffee and another coffee. An extra coffee was added to the list today – one plainly for luck. To be honest, mind, by this stage you have probably guessed that I wouldn't need any luck whatsoever (or would I?).

My train was to leave at 10.10am, giving me over three hours to get to the station. I felt like I could relax a little before making my journey south, but as those of you with kids would understand – half past nine and I was running late.

Although feeling naively positive that morning, there was still no real urgency to get to the station on time. It took some gentle persuasion from Jolie to get me there for my deadline, but, at 10.09am – there I was – Platform 7 – with my Walkman – waiting for my train.

As the 10.10 to Birmingham pulled in just a few minutes late, I started to vibrate. I really was vibrating – seriously! I was vibrating that much with nerves, that I could quite have easily vibrated all the way back home to the safety of my bed, and spent the rest of January 4, 2007 asleep – slaying robotic dragons in my dreams. But instead, I plugged my headphones into my nervous ears, and reluctantly stepped onto the train.

My overworking brain didn't even realise that the refreshment trolley passed me three times on the way to Birmingham, and by 11.30am I'd boarded my second train with Croydon being only a few hours away. Nevertheless, as we passed through the ever-changing countryside, my way of thinking gradually transformed itself from utter fear into slight apprehension. Soon after leaving Coventry, I began to experience weird feelings of excitement at the prospect of reaching my destination. It felt like I was sitting in a time-machine – on my way to another place and time, a place where I once loved to be, and a time in which things used to make perfect sense. As the train pulled up into East Croydon I couldn't wait to get off. Whilst walking up the ramp and through the station, old memories flooded my head as my eyes gazed upon things I'd not seen for years.

The cool, fresh air brushed my face when walking through the glass doors and onto the street, the sun shining above in the crisp blue sky. I stood on the corner next to the familiar tram-stop outside the station, watching the passers-by for a few minutes, when it suddenly dawned on me. What the hell am I doing here?

I hadn't really determined the answer to that question for the entire journey. Like I said earlier – January 4, 2007 was all Jolie's idea – not mine!

Still, as I pondered what my next move should be, a tram heading in the direction of my old workplace was pulling in. This seemed a golden opportunity to kill a few birds with one tram ticket. I clumsily rummaged through my pockets for loose change to feed the greedy ticket-machine before boarding the tram. It is always a good idea to get a ticket before boarding a tram in Croydon: the unpredictable inspectors can pounce at any stop. There is no escape!

Now, considering I'd made it onto the tram unscathed, I could only presume (in my slightly disoriented state of mind) that the bird which needed killing first was to have a look at the location where my old flat once stood. This bird to be followed by another brief journey up to *The Lodge* where I used to work as a chef, in the hope of getting some of the answers I so desperately needed. Jolie's idea was starting to show potential.

I felt quite at home as the tram pulled away from East Croydon, but I knew that home was not here anymore. Home was at home with my fiancée – no, sorry – girlfriend. That was another good thing that came from all this. If the voices never materialised, then I never would have met Jolie or her son Matty. Nor would I have my beautiful daughter Sarah, who is greatly adored by everyone. So, apart from saving me from perishing in the unforeseeable destruction of my flat, I also needed to thank the voices in person for giving me my family. But more importantly than thanking anyone, I just needed to find out from these wretched voices what the hell was going on. Maybe visiting the site of my old flat would hold some answers. Even though there couldn't possibly be anyone living there, deep down I kept hold of the thought that anything could be possible.

The tram was packed out with passengers, so even if any voices were trying to talk to me on this occasion, there was no way of distinguishing them from the other people on board. Besides, there were too many thoughts and memories rushing around my head to let the voices bother me. I didn't even have my headphones plugged in by this time. Instead, my eyes were concentrating on the world outside, taking in the various sights I thought I'd never see again.

While sitting alone on this heaving tram, I felt surprisingly calm venturing to the first destination on my list. However I did still feel slightly nervous about what events might be around the next few corners, but my eagerness to find out the truth seemed to displace any existing worries. However, as I stepped off the tram at my first port of call, my worries instantly took over my eagerness and I was left standing on the platform, facing the long straight road, leading to where I once lived.

I remained standing on that platform long enough for another two trams to pass as I stared down this daunting road; going over and over in my head the events that took place last time I was here. It seemed like an eternity ago, but I still remember the day clearly. I could picture myself hastily walking to the platform where I now stood, desperate to get away as the voices hurled abuse at me down the bitter street. It was a complete nightmare, a nightmare so terrible, that I never thought I'd be back, facing the same scene, but here I stood – it being January 4, 2007 – enacting Jolie's idea, not mine.

I put on my headphones and dubiously started to walk down the road towards my old abode. The flat used to be situated just around the corner, meaning that I couldn't see a thing until reaching the end of this ghastly street of horrors. My headphones would keep me protected for the time being, as I slowly made my way down the road; regressing further and further away from my safety net, the frequent trams behind.

Now, at this point, I would just like to say that if any of you are expecting big drum rolls and an explosive climax with regard to what I saw at the end of the road, then I'm afraid you're in for a huge disappointment. I finally made it to the end of Horror Street, looked left, only to see that there was nothing bloody there whatsoever.

I'd stood at that bloody tram stop for Lord knows how long, walked all the way down the road to hell, only to feast my eyes on a great big rectangle of tarmac with a few weeds protruding through the cracks – fantastic!

So what did I learn from that little expedition my mind wondered, as I stood there gaping at nothingness? Basically, the only thing to come out of such a colossal waste of time was that the news was right – my flat really did collapse. I mean, that little piece of information was discovered about two hundred miles away, from the comfort of my own bed!

As I headed back up the road from hell towards the tram stop, my phone rang. Mind you, I didn't hear it because I still had my bloody headphones on. It wasn't until I was on my way to try and kill another pointless bird, that I realised the instigator of the events of January 4, 2007 was just phoning to see if I'd made any progress. She phoned back.

"Progress?" I said. "Yeah, loads of progress baby – tons of the stuff."

"Oh that's good, Will," she replied. "What have you learned?"

"Well two things really," I said.

"What's that then, sweetie?" she asked.

"Firstly," I stated calmly, "you know my flat I told you about, the one which collapsed?"

"Yeah."

"Yeah, well guess what?"

"What?"

"It – really – really – did!"

"Did what?"

"Collapse, woman," I explained.

"Yeah well, I know that baby."

"Oh yeah. Well, guess what?"

"What's that baby?"

"So – do – bloody – I."

"Well that's good then baby," she concluded. "So are you having fun?"

"Fun?" I repeated, making sure there was no mistaking her question.

"Yeah – you know – fun, baby?" she asked again.

"Yeah, loads of fun baby – tons of the stuff," I answered, "in fact I'm not really sure which I'm getting more of – fun, or progress."

"See, I told you it would be worthwhile," said the proud 'instigator'.

"It's brilliant babe – really helpful," I replied sarcastically.

"Well I'm happy about that," she said patronizingly. "So what are you doing now?"

"Oh, I'm just sitting on a tram, darling, on my way to my old workplace, to see nobody I will recognise in all likelihood. You?"

"Nothing exciting, just tackling the out-of-control laundry pile we've managed to create in less than a week."

"Sounds like fun too," I said.

"Not as much fun as you must be having, I bet," suggested Jolie.

"Well, I wouldn't put any money on that just yet, gorgeous," I told her. "It's not all fun and games down here – trust me."

"Oh come on. You're telling me you'd rather be stuck in the house doing laun…"

"Sorry babe, I've got to go," I interrupted. "We're just landing at my stop."

"Oh all right then, well have a good time won't you."

"I'll try my best, sweetheart. Kids okay?"

"Yeah they're fine, baby. I'll probably see you tonight sometime then, I guess."

"Okay baby – speak to you later – love…"

"Oh wait, wait, wait – you didn't tell me the other thing you learned."

"Oh nothing much, baby. Just never – ever – ever – again – listen to any more of your ludicrous suggestions – that's all dear. Anyway, must dash – love you."

"Hey you cheeky little shit bag," she said in her more familiar tone, "you fucking better hope and pray that they give you your old job back down there, because you're going to need some pretty big balls if you think you're turning up here tonight... Will... Will... WILL... TALK TO ME YOU STUPID LITTLE ASS WIPE!"

I put my phone in my pocket and jumped off the tram, with my maiden smile of the day plastered across my previously impassive face.

*The Lodge* was just a couple of hundred yards up the hill from the tram stop. A short walk I'd made many times before, during my working days as a chef. The restaurant was located in a nice and peaceful setting, secluded from the busy main road and hidden by the tall, surrounding greenery.

That's as good as it got, though. It would be nice to be able to say that on my arrival, the fifteen-foot high golden gates automatically swung open: the impressive fountain display commenced, the harpists serenaded me, with relaxing and blissful song, as I promenaded up to the entrance across the pristine, velvet, red carpet; and the list of luxury treatments finished up with a man standing outside the front, in a smart suit and top hat, ready to hold open the door, and take my coat.

No such luck. As I waded through the deep gravel drive (half gravel – half cigarette ends) and up to the entrance, there was just one remotely positive thought on my mind. The remotely positive thing being, that at least *The Lodge* was still bloody standing!

Mind you, there were no more positive thoughts, other than that one microscopic detail. Apart from being terrified to step inside my old workplace, I couldn't help but think that I would be leaving this venue with about as much new information as I'd harvested from the assessment of the huge, rectangular, piece of tarmac where my flat used to sit.

Regardless of my mainly negative thinking, I still managed to pluck up the courage to walk through the front door and into the bar area. The barman was foreign to me, as were the various waitresses, carrying plates in and out of the kitchen to the few people dining in the restaurant (things had really gone downhill since I left).

You could just about see into the kitchen through the small glass window of the swinging door. But the glimpses I got of the chefs within, told me that these employees (along with everybody else) were part of a new breed of workforce, with their own little roles, to ensure Cioffi the general manager could still hover around his palace, wearing a fresh Armani suit each week.

Despite not recognising anybody, and nobody seeming to recognise me, it would have been quite nice to see Cioffi and have a little chat with him. It had probably been long enough since I left him in the lurch for him to forgive me, and besides – he could possibly be the one remaining person who could shed some light on my ambiguous situation.

But guess what? The barman informed me that Cioffi was in fact on holiday for a few weeks, so that was that. After finishing my pint, it looked like I'd be leaving *The Lodge* and Croydon too, without successfully killing any birds whatsoever!

I spent a few minutes walking through the restaurant, reminiscing and trying to find anything out of the ordinary, but everything just seemed – well – ordinary. I was the only one acting peculiar, as I moped around the restaurant with an empty pint glass. I was tempted to order some food but instead I decided to cut my losses and head back to the train station.

It was coming up to half past two when I left *The Lodge*: the sun was still shining and the air was still crisp. The harpists must have called it a day and the man with the top hat had run off with the golden gates. There were still no fountains, but plenty of time for some precipitation to occur instead.

As I waded back through the gravel carpet, I heard the crunch of footsteps heading towards me. A young woman in black trousers and a creamy cardigan was closing in. As she got close enough for me to distinguish her face, I thought that she looked familiar: the first familiar face I'd set eyes on all day. As she got closer, I was certain it was Siobhan: a waitress I used to work with. I was nervous at this point, but when she saw me walking towards her – she spoke first…

"Will – what are you doing round here?" she asked. "I haven't seen you for ages."

"Oh, I was just in the area," I replied. "Thought I'd pop in and have a look at the place."

"Well it's good to see you, Will," she said.

She pulled her hands from her cardigan pockets and gave me a big hug.

A Mental Note

Siobhan and I used to get on really well at work: we used to have a right laugh together – but that's as far as it went. She was seeing Toby for a while, the way Toby saw most waitresses for a while, in his own special way.

"So, are you still a waitress?" I asked.

"No I'm not, you cheeky git," was the answer. "I got promoted to restaurant manager a couple of years ago now, I'll have you know."

"Oooh – moving up in the world are we?" I joked.

"Not really," she said, "it's boring here now – not as fun as when you and Toby worked here, anyway."

"Oh well… So do you still see Toby at all?" I inquired. My mood shifted.

"Yeah, now and again," she replied. "He's head chef at *Flaming Ace* in town now – doing well, I think. What are you doing with yourself now, mate?"

There was a brief pause…

"Umm, walk a few dogs. Sorry – I've got to go, Debby – late for my train – bye."

"Oh, okay – bye. Oh, and Will…"

"Yeah," I said, as I headed across the drive.

"It's Siobhan – not Debby," she explained.

"Yeah, I know – see you later."

"Right – later it is then, I guess," she said, confused, and off she went to work.

Now then: if you think that my brief encounter with Debby – no, sorry, Siobhan – was the first time that Toby entered my head, then you'd be mistaken. He was my only known suspect, and seeing him could only prove to be beneficial.

Before I met Siobhan, there was no way of knowing how to get hold of him: no phone number: no address: no anything. Now I knew where he worked, making my visit to *The Lodge* a helpful occasion after all. Seeing Toby was going to be the best chance of finding out what was going on with me.

I crossed over the busy road and jumped on a tram for town: my new destination – *Flaming Ace*. This was going to be the biggest bird I'd try and kill all day! And if I wasn't going to kill it, it was certainly going to receive a thorough interrogation.

Watch out Toby: I'm on my way!

Look out Toby – I'm coming to get you…

*Interlude*

*"Talking pages"*

Have any of you tried writing a book? To be honest, I haven't really got a clue what the hell I'm doing! I would imagine that the obvious method to complete such a task would be to start at the beginning and work through till the end.

Not me though: that's far too rational for my brain. I mean I've already written the epilogue for pity's sake! Plus there's big chunks missing from the middle somewhere, making the whole task of writing this book that extra degree more difficult. Surely this is not normal - is it?

Marcus wants me to help him write a book about his experiences in the Army, as his writing skills are not one of his strongest attributes. Still, I'm sure, judging by some of the stories he has told me, it would make for an interesting read, nevertheless.

He's even thought up a name for his book. I was expecting something along the lines of '*Dangerous life*', or '*Pushing the limits*'. But no – nothing like this. Marcus wants to call his book '*Laughing in the face of farm machinery*'. Don't ask why. And yet he has always been a good one for telling stories, even though half the time they are just a made up pile of horse sugar. Maybe not so much now, but when he was a kid, he used to come up with some right beauties.

I think the best one I can recall off the top of my head, was the one he told us at the dinner table one Sunday round at mum's, about how he had been flying his kite one day, and suddenly this great big golden eagle flew straight through it and dropped dead in the field. Nobody could keep a straight enough face to finish their beef dinners after hearing that pile of cheese on toast.

Still, it's nothing short of pure entertainment when Marcus tells a story, so maybe it would be a good idea if he writes a book one day (or gets someone to write it for him). Who knows, maybe '*Laughing in the face of farm machinery*' will become a future best-seller?

It has been said in the publishing world that everybody has got a book inside them, but ninety-nine percent of the time – that's where it should stay! This doesn't sound like terrific odds by any means, so all I can do is hope that I'm one of the fortunate one percent. I'm definitely not, what some would describe as, 'normal', if that's any help?

I did have that publishing book to help me which I told you about earlier. That was until I left the damned thing on a train. The publishing book was in a rucksack, along with a bunch of DVDs, T-shirts and half a tub of powdered baby-milk.

Hear my advice. Don't leave your stuff on a train – ever! Even if your possessions do get lucky enough to make it to the main lost property department in Newport (South Wales), you probably won't find out because you end up having to report your list of misplaced items to a bloody answering-machine. You then have the privilege of spending the next seven to ten days, hoping that Pinocchio will turn into a real boy and phone you back. So that's what I'm doing at the moment, waiting. Surely there can't be too many rucksacks out there containing DVDs and baby milk?

Anyway I did have the publishing book in my possession long enough to learn a thing or two about writing a book. It had dawned on me when I started writing, that I really wasn't sure how many words a book should have, nor did I know how long a chapter should be, or how many chapters a book should have either.

Well, to my delight, the question, 'How long should a chapter be?' had a fairly straightforward answer. According to the publishing book, a chapter should be as long as it needs to be – as simple as that really.

As far as words go, well, I'm not going to worry too much and start counting them yet, but I do know there's bloody loads of them! And, by flicking through a selection of other novels, I have learned that some seem to contain relatively few chapters, while others have got over fifty of the things!

Now I know I'm not finished yet, but one thing's for sure. There won't be anything like fifty chapters in this book: it takes me long enough to write one, even with the two finger technique!

I guess what I'm aiming at is a happy medium. I definitely don't want to end up with a big fat chunky block that you could build prisons with, and I don't want to produce some farty little thing that you could read during one toilet-sitting (unless you happen to be extremely constipated).

Anyway, if this book is looking to be short of the mark, I could always beef it up a touch and throw in a few proverbs or word definitions. Maybe a couple of mindless quotations and a few pictures, not sure yet.

There is of course the opinion that size isn't everything. I happen to believe that some things can be too big and others too small (ladies – concentrate), but what's important is that you make what you've got count. I'm wise to the fact that I can't just write a load of old crap otherwise nobody will read it - will you? I guess for example it would be like me getting a pink and green striped suit tailor-made to fit my body perfectly. Well it might fit like a dream, but I'm still not going to bloody wear it – am I?

Right then, that's about it for now. 'Onwards and upwards,' as they say.

Wait a minute – what chapter am I on?

And on that note – let's get back to the programme.

## CHAPTER 14

## Flaming Toby

Off the top of my head, I'd say that *Flaming Ace* was probably so-called because it specialized in flame-grilled food, and the *Ace* part of the name was meant to support the belief that this flame-grilled food was, well, ace.

But the fact that Toby was now the head chef of this restaurant meant I was struggling to see how this could possibly be true.

Then again, to be fair, Toby always was a keen grill-chef when I think back to the time we used to work together at *The Lodge.* He even managed to grill that boiled egg I told you about before, so maybe Toby was actually a perfect candidate for the position.

I was going to find out!

It was approaching five o'clock when I finally made it to *Flaming Ace.* I'd decided to spend the preceding few hours wandering through the town centre, trying to find anything out of the ordinary, but all I found was the record shop where I pioneered my vinyl addiction.

I was slightly disappointed that the geezer who ran the shop failed to recognise me, especially considering half of my hard-earned wages usually found itself lining the inside of his till!

It was kind of a relief however, to learn that at least this bloke didn't seem to have any desire to destroy me, so I was able to remove him from my list of suspected tormenters.

I've got to be honest, my list wasn't any help whatsoever by this stage, due to the fact that previous theories concerning my voices had all gone up in a big puff of dark smoke.

Apart from my brief encounter with Siobhan back at *The Lodge*, plus the geezer at the record shop, I was struggling to find anyone else familiar, especially because Cioffi was off on his holidays and my old block of flats was no longer on the map. Toby was the one remaining 'bird' left who could be any help, and he was highly likely to be the one person who knew exactly what was going on.

This meant that a visit to *Flaming Ace* was the last card I had stashed up my sleeve; a highly vulnerable card given the uncertainty as to the cards in Toby's hand.

As I stood outside *Flaming Ace* I wasn't even sure if Toby was working, but if he was on the other side of those swinging doors, there was no way I could just walk up to him and start asking questions. This was a scenario that needed careful consideration before any action could be taken. I wasn't going to discover anything by standing outside, so, at about ten-past-five, I found the minerals and stepped into the premises.

At first I thought I'd just stepped inside a giant fruit machine! I'm sure the place was trying to replicate something, but I haven't got a clue what. The walls were furbished with huge flashing traffic lights, and great big mirror balls dangled from above. Multicolored party lights twinkled from corner to corner, and you simply couldn't escape yourself from the abundance of mirrors. It was more like being at a rave than a restaurant! Even the waiting staff patrolled the place in matching, yet eccentric, coloured uniforms. As I scoped out the venue, I feared that if I stayed here too long, I would end up with a bloody migraine! But one thing must have been true. The food had to be pretty edible because the place certainly wasn't short of customers.

I think it was Tina who greeted me at the front desk. Initially I was too bedazzled to remember to ask if Toby was working, and meekly assented when asked if I wanted a table for one. I was led to a table set for two, right next to the retro-styled jukebox in the corner of the restaurant. Tina then handed me a menu and informed me that a member of the waiting staff would be over shortly.

Now food wasn't really very high up on the priority list at this stage, but considering all I'd managed to eat was a piece of white toast whilst trying to get ready that morning, a proper meal was probably a good idea. So, I took the food list and parked my backside on the maroon cushioned chair, hoping that somewhere on this menu one could choose a sudden blackout and some strong painkillers!

To be honest, I wasn't interested in what there was to eat. The only thing on my plate was insatiable curiosity to know whether Toby was on the other side of those kitchen doors or not. Once I'd got my bearings, I observed the busy waiting staff as they ran plates of food through to the restaurant, looking like walking bowls of fruit salad! My mind was eager to find out who exactly was filling these plates. But as I sat there, still clutching my unread menu, I found it difficult to organize my thoughts into any kind of real order. My old best friend was possibly in the vicinity, but now I wasn't sure what he was. My views on Toby changed like the British weather every time I looked back to when we'd lived together. It was like he was on the end of a yo-yo, and now I'd managed to get myself completely tangled up.

It was quite tempting just to walk out before I ordered, to forget the whole thing, but something inside told me to stay put. I'd come this far, and walking out now would achieve nothing, so I remained calm and waited for some service. Service duly arrived around five minutes later. Kirsty's warm and friendly smile saved me from my headache, and momentarily brought me back down to Planet Earth. She asked if I would like a drink before I ordered my food, but, in-between answering her question, I managed to open a completely different discussion which gave me the opportunity to ask whether Toby was working or not:

"Toby, yeah Toby's working. Why, who shall I say is here?"

"Oh no nononono, it's okay, I was just wondering, that's all."

"Oh right, I see," said Kirsty. She continued smiling, still holding her pen and order-pad, waiting to find out what I would like to drink.

I just sat there agitated and confused as to what my next move should be. Kirsty had to prompt me once again to get an answer, clearly wanting to get on with her job.

So I answered:

"Do you do vodka?" I asked.

"We do indeed, sir," Kirsty responded.

"Great," I said. "I'll have a double."

"Okay sir, would you like anything with that?"

"Yeah, could you get me a pint of lager too, please."

"No problem," answered Kirsty. "Are we celebrating this evening?"

"I'm not sure yet, love," I said, trying to imitate something along the lines of a warm and friendly smile myself.

"I see, well I'll go and get your drinks and come back to take your order," explained Kirsty.

"Okay, thank you."

Kirsty ripped my drinks order from her pad and briskly headed over to the bar area. I was left sitting at my table with a heartbeat so rampant, even my blood was getting dizzy!

My eyes were now glued to the kitchen doors, full with the knowledge that either my best friend or worst enemy was somewhere on the other side. It wasn't until Kirsty returned with my pint and double vodka that I realized I still hadn't looked at my menu. So I asked her for a few more minutes to decide what to eat. I prised my eyes away from the kitchen doors and directed them at the food list.

At first, I might as well have been staring at a Japanese phone directory, because nothing was registering whatsoever, and yet, as my forty percent appetizer kicked in, my thought process became somewhat clarified. I was starting to relax.

I was still more preoccupied with thoughts of Toby than the prospect of hot food, but as I sat there, half reading, half reminiscing, my feelings towards him became harmless. I even started having a quiet little chuckle to myself when I thought back to some of the mischief we used to get up to, back at *The Lodge*.

Toby was without a doubt – one in a million. And the more I thought about the good times we had together, the more it seemed foolish to think he could ever be part of a plot to destroy my world. He was my friend for pity's sake – my best friend. He was probably the coolest bloke you could ever wish to meet. He was the 'Captain' for crying out loud, and not only that, he was in the next bloody room!

Now I was excited.

I'm not sure exactly what expressions I was pulling, but to other diners in the restaurant, it must have looked like I was actually overjoyed to have been stood up by my non-existent date. It would be fair to say that I was finding it really hard to control my excitement, but did my best to maintain normality. It was probably a bit like winning a grand on a scratch card whilst sitting in a library, and trying to keep your trap shut. However, any chance of being perceived as normal probably went flying out of the window as soon as I'd ordered my double vodka and a pint of larger.

But like I said – now I was excited.

"Do you do bubbly?" I asked Kirsty upon her return to my table.

"Bubbly?" repeated Kirsty.

"Yeah, you know, 'izzy wizzy let's get fizzy', and all that."

"Do you mean champagne, sir?"

"That's the stuff," I confirmed. "Bring me a bottle of your finest champers please."

Kirsty looked at me with a bemused expression, still holding her pen against her pad in the forlorn hope that I was about to order some food, given that this was *supposed* to be a restaurant.

"Sir, our most expensive bottle of champagne is nine-hundred-and-fifty pounds," she explained.

"Nine-hundred-and-fifty pounds you say," I answered, in a tone I thought might give the impression that this was a possibility. Now, maybe if I did win a grand on a scratchcard, then the purchase of such a delight might be within my grasp, but no – I hadn't, so no – it wasn't. Kirsty's sardonic smile revealed that she knew it wasn't possible either.

"I can bring you a glass of fizzy house wine, if would prefer, sir," she offered.

"Fizzy wine, you say."

"That's just if you prefer of course," clarified Kirsty.

"Well is it any good?" I queried.

"So I've been told," answered Kirsty with a grin.

"Okay then, if you insist," I resolved; "one glass of fizzy house wine."

"Very good sir," said Kirsty, who went on to ask; "and how about some food perhaps?"

"Food… of course," I said.

I re-engaged with the menu (still to be properly analyzed), only to stop reading as soon as I saw a picture of a tasty piece of gammon, with chips. To prevent any more time wasting, I concluded that gammon and chips would be a substantial belly-filler, so I went ahead and ordered:

"Can I have the gammon and chips please?"

"One - gammon - and - chips," Kirsty repeated as she jotted down my order on her pad.

"Yeah, surely he won't be able to cock that up too much," I muttered under my breath.

"I'm sorry sir – what was that?"

"Oh nothing, just talking to myself, sorry," I said, with a cheeky little smirk.

Kirsty looked back at me, probably attempting the impossible by trying to figure me out!

Really, the formal exercise of taking a simple food order, had turned into a charade by the time it came to ask me if I wanted egg or pineapple with my gammon. I was trying to keep one eye on the menu, one eye on Kirsty, and another on the kitchen door. (I should have gone to *Specsavers*.)

"Egg please," I requested.

"Okay sir, any side orders?"

"No, that will be fine thanks Kirsty," I concluded.

"Okay, I'll just get…"

"Oh, just one thing," I interrupted. "Could you ask Toby if he would kindly grill my egg?"

"Grill your egg!"

"Yes please."

"I don't think the chefs can grill eggs, sir."

"Trust me babe – Toby will know what to do."

"If you say so," said Kirsty, who took my order to the kitchen, leaving me with time to think about what I had just done.

The seed had now been planted. All that was left to do was to finish my pint and shit my pants!

Kirsty was taking her time in the kitchen, too. The inevitable discussion over the grilled egg gave me reason to metamorphose from pleasantly excited, to overwhelmingly panic stricken. Every time the kitchen door swung open, I buried my head behind my menu like an ostrich in the sand.

And then it happened.

I was a bit rusty in the art of teleportation, so instead I just sat there firmly embracing my pint of larger with one hand, my menu with the other, as this sweaty red forehead attached to a familiar spiky blond haircut, appeared from around the kitchen door. The tens upon thousands of flashing restaurant lights may as well have been replaced with one blinding spotlight, as Kirsty directed Toby's attention over to my table with her finger.

I was trapped! The damage had been done and there was no turning back. Luckily, someone else was cooking my dinner so at least the gammon was safe (apart from the pig of course). I didn't know whether to laugh or cry, walk over or run away. I opted to just stay put, and wait for Toby to make the first move.

Even though it was me who created the situation, it was definitely Toby who had control of it. He glanced over, trying to recognise the part of my face that wasn't hidden by my menu, but he had to fully step through to the restaurant to get a better view. Kirsty went over to the bar area, leaving a fully exposed Toby less than a stone's throw away. It was clear that he wasn't going to let the question of my identity rest, so I decided to skip the foreplay, and lowered my camouflage. Toby advanced closer and closer as I smiled at him from my seat, hoping that everything was going to be okay.

Now I'm not too sure if my appearance had changed that much since living in Croydon, or if Toby really should have gone to *Specsavers*, but it wasn't until he reached my table that the penny finally dropped.

He twigged, instantly, and everything was fine.

"Will! Bloody hell!" said a shocked Toby.

"Hello Captain."

"How the bloody hell are you?"

"Not too bad, mate."

"What the bloody hell are you doing here?" he asked.

"Why, is that okay?" I said defensively.

"Of course it's okay stupid. How are you?"

He offered me his hand to shake, which felt like being offered an Academy Award or something like that. As I took his hand, I felt the genuine warmth from his firm grip relax my senses and send me into a surreal, yet pleasant, comfort zone.

"How long has it been?" Toby asked.

"Must be seven years or so now, I think."

"Bloody hell, you haven't changed a bit, Will."

"Yeah I see you're still visiting the same barber, Toby."

"Yeah well, you know me Will: the ladies can't get enough of it son," followed by, "here, Will, what do you think of Kirsty?"

"Oh what, is that your missus?" I asked.

"Certainly is brother, isn't she a little minx?"

"Would that be the little minx you robbed from *The Lodge*?" I asked.

"Oh no, that was Jenny," he answered. "Why, who told you that?"

"Well, I spoke to Cioffi on the phone a while ago, trying to get hold of you," I explained.

"Ha ha, Cioffi, how is the Italian stallion?"

"Well he said he was going to kill you when he gets his hands on you."

"Yeah, well I'd like to see him try," said Toby, as he rolled up the sleeves of his not-so-white chef's jacket.

A few moments later, Kirsty came over to the table with her warm and friendly smile, and my glass of fizzy house wine.

"Ah," she sighed. "I should have guessed that you two would be friends."

"Kirsty darling," said Toby. "I want you to treat this gentleman like royalty, okay sexy?"

He put his arm around Kirsty's neck, and pulled her head in towards his chest, to make a statement of his masculinity. I took a sip of my fizzy cat's piss, and revelled in the couple's happiness, even though this waitress was probably just another one waiting to bite the dust.

Toby slapped Kirsty's bottom and sent her on her merry way. He then pulled up the seat reserved for my non-existent date, and sat down.

"Here, Will," he said in a quieter, more serious tone. "Did you hear about our old block of flats collapsing?"

"I did actually, yeah."

"Mad, isn't it?" he said.

"Yeah, you could say that," I answered, trying to glean information from his expressions.

"Yeah, well it's lucky you left really, because I couldn't afford the rent once you'd gone."

Suddenly, I slipped off my comfort perch and landed in a bowl full of sloppy guilt.

"Listen Toby, I'm so sorry about…"

"Will – Will – Will," he butted in, "honestly, it's fine."

I timidly looked at him to see if he genuinely accepted my half-apology, when he said:

"Look, I don't know what happened, but I could tell something wasn't right."

"You could?"

"Yeah, you did start acting a bit strange."

"Yeah well…"

"Look, Will, what are your plans? Are you staying here for a while?"

"I'm not really sure, Captain," I said. "I was going to get a train home once I've eaten."

"No sod that," insisted Toby. "Look, I've got to go back to work now, but I'm finished at ten. If you want, you can stay at mine tonight and we'll have a chat, yeah."

"Okay," I accepted, "that would be good."

"Sorted then," said Toby. "Kirsty will take care of you anyway, and I'll just be in the kitchen if you want me."

"Okay, thanks Toby," I said, and once again shook his hand.

Toby then got up and left the restaurant to check on his team of monkeys and my piece of gammon. I let off a big puff of steam and readjusted myself to my new environment. No more was I a dateless alcoholic, but a V.I.P guest on first-name terms with the head chef.

I smiled, looked down and straightened out my cutlery. The order had been given to look after me, and support was there if at all required. I sat there and waited patiently for my gammon.

Boy I'm hungry!

**CHAPTER 15**

**Episode one too many**
**Episode Two**


I was impressed: the kitchen crew had been trained well. Toby's predecessor must have done a very good job training them. My gammon was succulent, tender and crisscrossed like a palatable chess board. My chips were chunky, crispy and eye-pleasingly golden, and they had even managed not to grill my egg! Even the side salad looked half tempting.

Until I moved in with Jolie, salad would not even make it onto my fork, let alone into my mouth, if I was ever presented with such a flavourless waste of space.

But then Jolie taught me a recipe for some salad-dressing that converted me into a full-blown rabbit overnight. Now I can't get enough of the stuff, so long as it's swimming in Jolie's dressing.

Unfortunately, I forgot to pack some of this wondrous dressing that morning, so I tucked into my gammon, egg and chips, and left my side salad where it usually belongs – on the side.

As I dunked one of my beefy chips into my scrumptiously runny egg yolk, the sparkle from all the coloured lights across the restaurant, took me back to a holiday with my mum and dad in Blackpool as a kid.

Now, if it felt like I was dining inside a giant fruit-machine at *Flaming Ace*, then I suppose Blackpool can only be described as one of the biggest one-arm bandits on the planet! Probably a bit like Vegas, but with more doughnuts! The annual illumination shows hosted in Blackpool enhance the whole atmosphere of the place, as each of the thousands upon thousands of light bulbs do their bit to attract some of Britain's most eccentric holiday-makers.

But these mesmerizing light-shows come at a price. The annual bill to host the illuminations is well in excess of two-million pounds! Probably not the most environmentally-friendly show on earth, and I would have thought that coastal resorts would want to do their best to keep sea levels down! Have you ever heard the phrase – '*All good things come to those who wait*?' Well, what a load of bollocks that is. Try telling that to someone who's on Death Row (don't worry Blackpool – not you).

Sorry, I'm getting a bit excited. I'll be running for Prime Minister next. To be fair, I can't really do much worse a job – surely?

"Probably a bit of a long shot that one, Will. Maybe go down the Jobcentre when you get back to Shrewsbury, and see if there's any part-time positions working for the Illuminati, instead."

Don't get me started on the Illuminati, please. I've barely started scratching the surface, but I know the secrets run deep!

Anyway, what was I doing? Oh yes, dunking a beefy chip into my scrumptiously runny egg yolk.

Yeah – nice chip…

Sorry I'm miles away. I'm having trouble focusing at the moment.

Okay… so I ate my chip…

Yeah, so as I was eating my dinner the place started getting even busier. The time was approaching six-thirty and I thought it best to give Jolie a quick tinkle and inform her of my new plans.

Fortunately, she had calmed down since our last phone call and was happy that I'd run into Toby and was making progress. It didn't come as any shock to her that nobody was trying to kill me, and she encouraged me to take as much time as I needed, if it was to be beneficial towards ending my ordeal.

I was only too willing to accept Jolie's offer for a bit of space away from screaming kids, but assured her I'd be back sometime next day. I hung up the phone, polished off my dinner (minus the salad), and had a think about dessert.

"What would you suggest?" I asked Kirsty as she came to clear my table.

"How about a soft drink this time?" she proposed.

"No, I mean for dessert, silly."

"Well, the cinnamon-swirl cheesecake is pretty yummy, I suppose," suggested Kirsty.

"Yeah, that does sound good," I agreed. "Go on then, give us one of those."

"Okay shag," she said with a wink. "One cinnamon-swirl cheesecake coming up."

Now there was Toby telling Kirsty to treat me like a V.I.P, and I'd just been demoted from "sir" to "shag." Talk about cheek! Mind you, she did redeem herself by bringing me the sweetest, sexiest cheesecake I have ever had the pleasure to taste.

She offered me some extra-squirty cream (just in case there weren't already enough calories). Out of the blue, she shook the bottle provocatively trying to entice me to have a huge blob. It would be fair to say that ever since Toby had gone back to the kitchen, this waitress was definitely flirting.

So, "Squirt away," I offered.

"Where do you want it?" she said, with a teasing tone to her voice.

"All over the place," I suggested.

So she lent down and started to saturate my plate with cream. I had to use physical force to prevent this girl from getting carried away! Even though she didn't use her tongue to clean off any excess cream from the nozzle, I surprisingly did get the impression that Toby might have met his match with this little player.

Once Kirsty left me to enjoy my pudding, I began by taking tiny, spaced-out, mouthfuls due to the fact that I had about three hours to kill before Toby finished work. However, the act of taking tiny, spaced-out, mouthfuls of something so delicious became simply too torturous for me to keep up, and my cinnamon swirl cheesecake, with half a can of squirty cream, was doomed just minutes later.

So, after a brief conversation with myself in the washroom, I returned to my table and ordered a coffee. Not just a normal coffee but an Irish coffee: an Irish coffee with extra Irish! Actually, as I was a VIP, it meant that there wasn't much room for coffee in my coffee, because of Kirsty's more potent additives, and her clear fondness for cream.

Now as I sat there, slurping on this hot and hazardous beverage, a beaming smile across my face, I felt a certain satisfaction with my day's efforts. My encounter with Toby had positively reassured me that he was innocent, and knew sweet Jack sugar about my voice situation. The reception I received from everybody else I met that day could only be described as positive also. Kirsty was doing a good job keeping me happy in my newfound comfort zone, and my family was back at home waiting for my safe return next day. It was the start of a new year and I felt fantastic. In fact, you could say that I was back on top of the world.

But, as I told you before – when you're sitting on top of the world, it's a long way down! The view was great from my table: the flashing lights and happy diners were delight to my eyes. But I didn't notice the black ice beneath my feet, waiting for me to slip without warning.

Yes, I was in a comfort zone, but this was an unfamiliar area to be in: a comfort zone created by strangers, and a person who had been playing with my mind, causing uncertainty, for years.

Yes, Toby had managed to fill me with reassurance, but as I've found over the years, reassurance only works in the presence of the reassurer. I knew Toby was only in the kitchen next door, but believe me when I say that this was far enough away for the reassurance to collapse and come crashing down on me, eradicating all my good feelings.

And that's exactly what happened – I slipped and fell. Unfortunately, I wasn't even wearing a parachute, and before I could say, "One more Irish coffee, please," I crash-landed in an alien station, full of scheming antagonists.

Whilst sipping my coffee, observing my surroundings, I started catching glimpses of people staring at me from their tables. Kirsty still smiled at me as she walked to and from the kitchen, but now her smile didn't seem as warm and friendly as before. Now it was just a deceptive visage to hide the truth from me.

But I wasn't falling for the ruse: I knew what was going on. She was spying on me, and then sending information back to Toby in the kitchen as he plotted what he was going to do to me later that evening.

I started putting some possibilities together inside my head, and I started to panic.

"Maybe he already has done something. Maybe he got the kitchen staff to drug your meal! In fact, is that them laughing next door?"

I looked around the restaurant as I mumbled to myself, determined to find more evidence that something fishy was going on.

"There – table four. They've got a role in all of this. He just blatantly stared at you Will. In fact, look around, everyone's smiling and laughing! They all know what's going on. Yeah, that's why the place is so busy, because you're here. They want to see you in the flesh, Will. In fact, they must have known you were coming so they must be watching you somehow. Shit! That's why Kirsty keeps flirting with you; she wants you to do something wrong so Toby batters you! I wonder if Jolie's at home watching all of this on the telly with her mates. No, surely Jolie can't know anything about all this – can she Will? Oh please don't say you are Jolie – I need you."

A quick mental calculation of the equation of my situation: Toby plus Kirsty)/diners, minus chicken pie, came to the grand total of 'Need to pay the bill, and get the hell out of here, pronto!'

But, before I could move, I had to assess the consequences of what might happen if I did leave. It was fast becoming clear that the longer I stayed, the more people would realize where I was.

"Careful, Will, there might be a trap for you outside. But the longer you stay here, the more likely you're going to get hurt. Oh no – someone please help me."

Then along came the voices. They were in the bloody restaurant – I could hear them.

"*Ha ha, he doesn't know what to do, does he?*"

"*Fuck him, just let him stew.*"

"Where are you?"

"*Oh piss off Will. You're going to get a right pasting when you leave here.*"

"What, can you see me?"

"*Everyone can see you, dickhead.*"

"Where are you?"

"*Look Will, I suggest you go before you get hurt.*"

"*Yeah, nobody wants you here anyway.*"

"I'm not doing anything wrong, am I?"

"*Shut up you idiot.*"

"*Hey Will, guess what. I'm at your house at the moment, in bed with your girlfriend.*"

"No you're not."

"*Why do you think she wanted you out of the way?*"

"She's trying to help me."

"*Nobody's trying to help you Will: everybody's just laughing at you.*"

"*Yeah, why would Jolie want anything to do with a prick like you?*"

I pulled my walkman out and plugged in to try and muffle the voices, but they were too strong. Not only that but now I was afraid of what I might not hear too. I was running out of options fast, but action had to be taken.

I unplugged my headphones and had a think:

'Right Will, just work out how much the bill comes too and leave the money on the table, okay.'

As calmly as possible, I read through the menu and made a mental calculation of my bill. I then slyly pulled my wallet from my back pocket, so as not to let anyone see what I was about to do, but this didn't work either!

"*We know what you're doing Will.*"

"*Yeah do you think we're stupid?*"

"I'm not doing anything."

"*Yes you are, you're going to run away.*"

"How do you know that?"

"*Because we can hear your thoughts stupid.*"

Suddenly I froze. Now I was really terrified. Could people really hear me thinking?

In my state of panic, I tried to decide if this was really possible. The only way to find out was to speak out silently, and wait for a reaction.

"Listen you bunch of pricks, you're all sad and ugly, and I wouldn't piss on you if you were on fire," I imagined.

"*Oh Will, You're in so much trouble now.*"

"*Will, you're a fucking dead man.*"

Once again I froze. It was really happening: people could hear my thoughts.

"What, you can really hear me thinking?"

"*Of course we can, you idiot.*"

"*Ha ha, he didn't even realize did he.*"

"I don't believe this."

"*Well you better believe it, you prick.*"

"*Yeah, and you better believe that you're not going to make it out of Croydon alive, you fucking idiot.*"

By this time, it must have swiftly become apparent to any diners out of the loop, that there was something seriously amiss at my table, as I sat there fidgeting with menus, empty glasses, cutlery and anything else to hand. Every time a door opened, I jolted in my seat in literal fear for my life.

There was only one thing left to do in such a dangerous situation. I had to phone Jolie. Mum didn't even know where I was: she wouldn't have wanted me to come to Croydon in the first place. So Jolie was my only hope. But the hope was that Jolie wasn't part of the malicious plan to have me killed. After all - this day was actually her idea.

Amongst the mayhem, I nervously pulled out my phone and started dialing.

"Come on, come on, answer your phone," I urged.

"Hey baby, everything okay?"

"Jolie where are you?"

"I'm at home sweetie, are you okay?"

"Who are you with?"

"Nobody. Why? What's wrong?"

"What are you doing?"

"I'm just getting the kids ready for bed, why, what's the matter?"

"So there's nobody there with you?"

"No Will, are you okay?"

"No I'm not okay, I think I'm in trouble."

"Why, what have you done?"

"I don't know."

"Well, where are you?"

"I'm in the restaurant still."

"So what's gone wrong?"

"Well people are going to kill me I think."

"Okay, okay, just calm down and tell me what to do, yeah."

"I don't know but is it okay if I come home please?"

"Don't be silly, of course it is sweetie."

"Okay I will, but I'm stuck in the restaurant at the moment."

"Okay Will, listen to me. Stay on the phone and I'll talk you through what to do, okay."

"Okay, thanks Jolie."

And thank the lord she did. She talked me through leaving enough money on the table and walking out. She talked me through the walk to the train station, and she talked me through the act of stepping onto the train.

By the time I got to Birmingham, I was at ease enough to make the rest of the journey unaided, so I told Jolie that I would see her back at home a few hours later.

That was the last time I ever visited Croydon, and probably the last time I would ever see Toby again.

As I sat on the train from Birmingham, with my headphones on, I tried to figure out what went wrong, but, like normal, I could find no logical answer. One thing I did know, Croydon was most definitely a chapter in my life that should be put to rest. Another thing I realized was that I really did need some proper help. Not the odd tablet here and there, I mean professional help.

The more I thought about the evening's experience at *Flaming Ace*, the more it seemed apparent that all the danger I felt was just a creation of my mind.

Considering the fact that I walked out on Toby all those years ago, I couldn't really have asked for a warmer welcome back. Maybe if I'd just gone and got him from the kitchen, like he said I could, then all of this could have been prevented.

And Kirsty? She was just doing her best to make me feel good. She wasn't flirting, she was just being friendly.

And all those diners? People go to restaurants to have a good time, not just to sit there and mope. That doesn't mean they came to laugh at me: they don't even know me!

'This is stupid, Will. You need to go and see your psychiatrist and tell him what's going on. You can't carry on like this anymore: you've got kids to think about now. Yeah, get home and sort it all out. You're okay Will, okay. Jolie's going to look after you and everything's going to be fine – I promise.'

**CHAPTER 16**

**The Real Prick of Destiny**


"Okay William, I'm going to count to three, and on three, I want you to take a deep breath and relax – understand?"

"Go for it."

"Here we go then, one, two..."

It was January 22, 2007, and I was lying face down on my bed, with the top of my buttocks slightly exposed above my unzipped jeans.

But before all that, let's roll the tape back a week or so to the appointment with my shrink.

It was actually Jolie who got the ball rolling and booked this appointment. Now, an appointment with a psychiatrist was hardly a new concept but, this time, I was going in with a fresh outlook on my situation.

You could say that my last trip to Croydon was the final straw really. I was sick and tired of going through life, trying to find a solution to a seemingly unanswerable question. It appeared that I was wasting my time.

Mum and Eric knew this, Dad knew it, the doctors knew it and even Jolie knew it too. Even though Jolie was open-minded and understanding, she simply couldn't bear to see me go through such torment anymore. Jolie instructed me to be truthful with my psychiatrist and tell him everything, including the fact that I wasn't taking my medication properly.

There were a few reasons why I didn't like taking my tablets. Firstly, I was terrible at remembering to take a tablet every day anyway. But I also didn't like taking these daily tablets because it was a constant reminder that something wasn't right. And the fact that my family constantly asked me if I *had* taken one of these bloody tablets just made everything even worse.

I was also afraid that these tablets were somehow designed to make me forget, and blind me from, the truth about what was really happening to me. After all, they did knock me for a hefty six!

Anyway, such a long time had elapsed without the aid of medication, and I'd spent so many years convincing myself that my 'mental note' was right: dealing with my voices simply became part of everyday living.

But was my mental note right?

Well, my block of flats did collapse. But if the voices were trying to warn me of this, then why did they have to be so horrible sometimes?

And if I was being monitored – how was this possible? And how could I hear the voices?

To be honest, there isn't much I'd put past technology these days. I certainly know there's some pretty sophisticated surveillance kit out there, but why pick on me? There's nothing fantastically special about my life that would interest people on a daily basis, surely?

But I'd told myself in the beginning that, no matter what the future might hold, my 'mental note' was right and I was sticking to it!

Oh, I don't know anymore. I better go and have that chat with my psychiatrist.

"So, how can I help you William?"

"Well, the truth is Doc, that I haven't been taking my medication."

"I see, and why's that?"

"I don't know really."

"Don't you think you need medication, William?"

"To be honest, I don't know anymore."

"I see."

"Yeah, well I just wanted to see what my options are really."

After an hour or so of heartfelt discussion, it was decided that I would undergo a fortnightly depot injection program, which would be carried out at my home by a qualified nurse. The injection consisted of the same medication I'd been prescribed seven years ago in tablet form, but having this injection was like taking two weeks' worth of tablets, without having to constantly think about it.

This proposed treatment was to be an intramuscular injection, administered directly to the backside. When the shrink told me that the nurse would alternate bum cheeks every two weeks, I couldn't help but giggle. I sat there thinking I could tell which week it was by the plasters on my ass.

I was still a bit dubious about this new proposal, especially when I first saw the size of the bloody needle!

Apparently, this form of treatment was designed by Americans, and due to America's general population of (how can I say this without causing offence?) substantial butts, the needle had to be so long, just to reach the target muscle!

So yeah, on January 22, 2007, the nurse came to my house. I was only mildly offended that this lady brought two male nurses with her, who were blatantly there as back-up, just in case I lost the plot or something. It doesn't take three people to give one injection, surely? But the real problem was that we were running low on teabags! Jolie was out shopping with the kids, so I was left at home doing the entertaining. None of the nurses took me up on my offer of a cold glass of water, so we got straight down to business.

We were all sat in the kitchen on the second floor, discussing my injection. As the female nurse explained the procedure whilst drawing up the milky coloured fluid, I couldn't help but think that somewhere hidden in this dose, was another bloody tracking-device!

"There isn't a tracking-device hidden in there, is there?"

"No don't worry William, just a dose of the good stuff, I promise."

"So, you lot aren't secret agents then?"

"Afraid not William, we're just plain old nurses."

"Oh, that's alright then."

"So where do you want me to give you this?" the nurse asked.

"Well, it's supposed to go in my backside isn't it?"

"Yes, but do you want to stand up in here, or would lying on the bed be more comfortable for you?"

"Okay, well, we can go up to the bedroom then."

"Right then, well, this is ready, so lead the way William."

I escorted Tom, Dick and Nancy up to the bedroom on the third floor, and followed instructions to lie face down on the bed and lower my trousers slightly.

And that brings us back, just in time, to the beginning of this chapter:

"… three."

"AAAAAAAAAAAAAAAGGGGGGHHHH!"

Only joking: I hardly felt a thing. Well I did feel something I suppose, but nothing near as bad as say, plucking a nasal hair in slow motion.

And then it was over for a whole two weeks. I didn't cry and I didn't lose the plot.

I think the female nurse took quite a shine to me, and made various positive suggestions after seeing some of my artwork on the wall. She seemed impressed when I told her that she could go and visit the trendy little wine-bar in town I told you about; the walls of which were, by now, dominated by some of my crazy creations.

She even came two weeks later, minus one nurse (Dick). Obviously I wasn't so much of a threat after all.

And that's pretty much that. I've been having these fortnightly injections ever since, and I can't fault them. They really have done me the world of good. The voices have virtually faded away, and all paranoid thoughts have evaporated. I still have the odd bad day, but then again, so does everyone.

When I look back now, some of the things I used to believe seem totally ridiculous. I really can't believe I carried on believing them for so long, when it could all have been so easily prevented.

I still feel that the voices saved my life, but it wasn't really that people were warning me my flat was going to collapse: it was just a coincidence – that's all. I know that now.

Like so many things that have happened in my life since Croydon, it has just been too easy to perceive these things in a totally irrational way, and come up with a completely ludicrous explanation.

Two plus two does not add up to sixty-four – nowhere bloody near! The grass is green and the sky is blue (well, that's debatable in Britain I suppose). But you get my point. It probably sounds silly to someone who hasn't experienced a mental illness themselves, but believe me – it's no joke.

Anyway, like most problems in life, there is usually an answer, and I finally found mine and I've never looked back.

And that pretty much concludes this work. I think I've covered everything.

Well… not quite…

**CHAPTER 17**

**Croydon**

"Are we doing the business boys?"

"Of course we are, Cioffi. Toby, where's that side-salad? This table's waiting to go."

"I'm on it boss."

"Siobhan, can you start taking these to table twelve please: let's go, let's go, let's go."

"One side-salad, chef."

"Great stuff Captain: next order – two chicken, one mixed grill, four beef. Let's bang them out boys…"

I was on the top of my game: I was Cioffi's golden boy. A full restaurant was a walk in the park for me, as I stood in front of a grill full of sizzling meat, absorbing the pressure like a sponge.

"Garnish boys, don't forget the garnish."

"We're on it, Cioffi."

"Will, you are the business, the bloody business son."

I was fast, really fast – bloody fast! I could churn out three-hundred meals on the busiest nights of the week and hardly break a sweat.

It was a complete contrast to when I first started working at *The Lodge*. To begin with, I was a total liability. Late for the breakfast shift; late for the evening shift; never set for service; whipping waitresses with tea towels and so on. I nearly lost my job on numerous occasions, and even got suspended from work for a week!

I suppose I was just trying too hard to enjoy myself, and I prioritized the fun things in life over my job.

Put it this way. On my days off, you certainly wouldn't catch me sitting at home comparing Meerkats! I was always busy looking forward to the next night out, or the next big thrill in life, to be worried about anything else. I was on a wild rollercoaster, going a hundred miles an hour with a blindfold on, meaning, I didn't really know what I was doing or where I was going.

But all this wild partying was having a deeply negative impact on my work. I'm sure you can imagine that a hot and busy kitchen is not the best place to be with a stinking hangover.

The waiters and waitresses thought it was funny to see me constantly landing myself into trouble, which I suppose just fuelled me more so to make them laugh. Essentially, my job was just a big joke to me, and I was a joke to everyone else.

But Cioffi wasn't laughing – far from it. I was on thin ice, and it was starting to crack. My livelihood, as well as my home, was in jeopardy, and my whole life in Croydon was swiftly becoming a disintegrating dream.

But then something happened. At the time it was probably the best thing that could have happened, but in the long run it was most definitely the worst!

You would probably think that the only way to get into Cioffi's good books would be to stop the wild nights out drinking, and focus more on my job instead.

But this is only half the truth.

Instead of putting the brakes on and taking my blindfold off, I just went faster and faster on my wild rollercoaster. In fact, I started going so fast, I nearly doubled back in time!

The nights got wilder and wilder, and the parties got even harder. I stayed up later and later, until that's all I really did – stay up. Sleep became scarcer and scarcer, until I practically forgot what it was like to dream!

I'm serious! There really was no time for sleep anymore, especially when there were plenty more exciting things to do – like being awake. And the best thing about all this wakey-wakey time was that it didn't affect my work whatsoever.

Well, actually that's rubbish; my work was affected, but not in a bad way. I knuckled down and very quickly became an important member of staff, and a considerable asset within the kitchen team. I received a promotion from starter chef to grill chef, plus a nice little pay rise for my efforts. I became the star in Cioffi's eye as he regularly told me that he was taking me all the way. This could only have meant good things for my future at *The Lodge*.

And what was it that was allowing all of this to be possible?

Well, you should know the answer to that by now.

Amphetamine – speed – lemonade – whatever you want to call it: lots of it, too!

Don't worry, really it's safe to drink lemonade, but as I was going to find out, it most definitely isn't safe to take speed – especially the amount I was taking. I won't go into the ins-and-outs of it all, but it was a lot! Enough to hold down a hectic fulltime job and to do it well, enough also to live a completely separate life with virtually zero rest. The busy evening kitchen shifts just got me pumped up enough, so I could do whatever I felt like in my newfound nocturnal time off.

And I was never late for breakfast anymore. How could I be? I never went to bed! I was fast in the kitchen and always ready for service. I was always on the ball during service and my improvement was duly noted.

I even enjoyed my work more, especially after I started to gain the respect from my fellow workmates, and especially from the general manager.

Cioffi was very pleased with my improvement, saw the potential to produce a great chef, and gave me incentives to do even better. At one point it felt like I was receiving phantom tax-rebates left, right and centre for all my hard work. Whatever challenges were set I rose to them with flying colours, and thrived off the praise I received.

The trouble was, and this is hardly an excuse, that Cioffi expected this level and standard of work to continue, but he didn't realize that my turnaround was due to the fact that I was always fully-charged on go-go juice!

Don't get me wrong, I enjoyed being able to work fast with unlimited energy supplies: I would to this day like to have that energy permanently. I would get a lot more done for one thing, and it is always nice to have a spring in your step.

But like I said earlier; what goes up, must come down. My spring turned to winter as my rollercoaster life slipped out of control. Eventually the wheels came loose and I went flying off the tracks, crash-landing in a completely different theme park. Unfortunately for me, there was only one ride in this park – the haunted house. A haunted house with no bloody exit: a frightening place to be when you're all on your own.

If I had known then what I know now, I would certainly have reconsidered ever taking such a dangerous drug, especially for so long. I was too busy wallowing in success to see the terrifying dangers lurking ahead.

And so it hit me: hit me like a bulldozer, so hard, that I didn't have a clue what was happening. It was the most frightening experience of my life, and I wouldn't wish it upon anybody.

Overnight, my entire existence turned into a completely messed up Rubik's cube. Reality as I knew it completely dissolved, leaving me in a place where nothing made any sense, and the sense I did make of the situation was actually completely false.

My brain had taken a thorough battering from chemicals and sleep deprivation, until my mind was completely shot! I simply couldn't keep up with myself anymore. Like the body, the brain needs rest so it can function properly, and I had driven my brain up to, and over, its limit.

The brain operates like a computer, but it's a computer far more complex than any device man could ever build. And if this computer crashes, unfortunately you can't just push a few buttons or take it to a shop to get fixed – it's not that simple.

So yeah – if you want my advice – conserve your mind! You've only got one and it's a precious tool. It is after all – you!

So if you're happy being you, then I would try and make sure that you stay being you – and not imitate me.

I was only too happy being me. It was great, never feeling tired and always being active. It was also great to be so admired for my work and to have the respect that supplemented this admiration. It was great having Toby as a best friend and living with him in our old flat. In fact, everything was great. But that was the old me, and because of my reckless lifestyle, I was forced into living a new life as a new person.

I won't lie to you, it was a terribly tough challenge getting used to a new life as a new me. It was equally tough for the people around me (especially my family) to adjust to this new me. I would imagine they must have felt weak and powerless, being in a situation they had no control over.

But over time, things got easier, and now I have a lot to look forward to. I have a family of my own now, and am privileged to be able to see my children growing up.

Family life is an eventful life, and I'm sure there will be good days as well as bad ones. But like I said – everyone has bad days. If we didn't have bad days sometimes, then how could we possibly appreciate the good times?

So yes, you could say that I once lived in a world of stinking sugar, but still managed to come out smelling sweet on the other side.

One thing that still plays on my mind to this day though is wondering what might have happened if I'd never become ill. There is always that unnerving possibility that I could have suffered the same fate as my old block of flats, if I hadn't been forced to change. In a way you could see it as a blessing in disguise, becoming ill, but the truth of the matter is, I'll never know.

Now and again I also spend time wondering what sort of person I would have turned out like if things were different. But I'll never know the answer to this question either, so I suppose it's a pointless task thinking too hard.

It's ironic in a way, because my problem has always been the same – I don't think – I just do, and now I wish I didn't. Well I don't anymore because I'm too busy thinking. However, this excessive thinking usually ends up with me getting my twist in a pants (see what I mean?).

Even though I feel well again, I'm sure that the events in Croydon have left me with a pretty weird and wonderful outtake on life. I'm not sure if this is a good thing or a bad one, especially when people don't seem to have the faintest idea what I'm talking about half the time. Surely I'm not that strange – am I?

Anyway, originality is the spice of life, and I'm hotter than Marcus' chilli pizza. Then again, it's questionable as to whether that bloody pizza was a good thing or not. Put it this way, I certainly wouldn't eat one just before my injection, otherwise it would be the nurse getting the dose – not me!

"Stop thinking, Will."

Well that pretty much wraps Croydon up in psychoactive wrapping-paper and not-so-fancy ribbons. Mum was wrong. There was nothing wrong with Croydon: there was something wrong with me. I'm not sure if Mum fails to see the bad in me, or simply just refuses to. Whatever the truth is, I love my mum and am eternally thankful to her for putting up with someone who is sometimes so difficult.

It's different with Eric. Eric secretly buzzes off my wrongdoings. It gives him ammunition if ever his son, Marcus, does something wrong, as, in those instances, it is Mum doing all the buzzing.

To be honest, both Mum's and Eric's guns are fully loaded in their little immature 'battle of the sons'. If only they knew what the lads got up to in the army! It would be Mum carrying the weapon of mass destruction if that was the case.

Really though, Mum doesn't need any weapons in an argument with Eric. Mum's verbal bullets are sufficient to leave Eric eating his words, licking his wounds, and retiring into submission. And once that event has happened, it's aimless for Eric to continue, because once you've eaten your words – you just end up talking shit!

I know; I'm getting sidetracked like normal. I've told you about Croydon, haven't I? Basically you know everything there is to know: the whos, the whats, the whys, the wheres and the when. Unlike Mum and Eric, I'm completely out of bullets.

Oh hang on – isn't there one left in the chamber?

**CHAPTER 18**

**Coming Clean**


So here we are folks, the last chapter, the conclusion of this work, the point where everything is supposed to come together, nice and neat and tidily. But I've got to be straight with you, this grand finale can't really be all that neat and tidy, quite simply, because my 'mental note' was wrong. You already know that people weren't trying to destroy my world or play an incredibly high-tech joke on me of some description, and you know that the reason for me believing these things was because of drugs.

So what am I supposed to say? Don't do drugs! Well that's an obvious statement to make for a thousand different reasons and no matter how much you try and put drugs down, it will never change the fact that they will always be out there, in every town, in every city, on every street, and it's naive to think otherwise. Like pretty much everything else on this crazy planet, it all boils down to money and there is just too much money to be made in the narcotics industry for there ever to be an end, because the demand for drugs is just too high. Maybe money does make the world go round after all.

Everyone already knows that drugs are bad so what's the point in me telling you? But what do most people do if something is bad? I'll tell you what. They sweep it under the carpet and pretend it's not there. Well, considering there are so many drugs out there to sweep up, unless you happen to possess a pretty enormous super-brush, then I think you'll find that that's a pointless little exercise too.

Of course drugs are bad, but that doesn't mean that all people who take them are bad. I guarantee that at some point in everyone's life, they are going to come into contact with drugs, somewhere, somehow. This means, people, that one day, your kids and my kids are probably going to end up making a choice, and, unfortunately, no matter how much you think you are in control, drugs have the power to grab hold of and destroy even the best of people, and that is a fact!

And that goes for all drugs. It's not just speed that has the potential to ruin lives. There are plenty of other illicit substances out there, just waiting to take down their next helpless victim. Trust me, I've seen it happen to too many people, and the trouble is that once you go down that road, it's extremely difficult to find a way back.

So in saying this, wouldn't it be better if we all understood drugs instead of pretending they don't exist? It's not as if you've got to go to university to study them or anything like that. Just reading a few leaflets would educate us enough so that one day, if we are asked anything about drugs by our kids, we might have something a bit more constructive to say than "just stay away."

Well, I think that's all I'm going to say on the subject. How about a little discussion on mental health?

Of course I'm no psychiatrist so I can only really comment on my own experience. I know that coming to terms with having a mental illness has probably been the hardest part for me. It would have made things a lot easier, I'm sure, if the doctors could have proved to me in black and white that I was mentally ill, instead of me having to take everybody's word for it.

I also know that I should have taken my medication properly a long time ago. I mean, taking half a tablet, sometimes, maybe, just isn't good enough. Medication is medication and it is prescribed to people for a good reason, as I learned after undergoing my injection programme.

It is likely that I will have to receive this fortnightly injection for the rest of my life, but really this is a small price to pay if it makes me feel well, and keeps those menacing voices at bay.

Ah yes, the voices. I'd better give those assholes a mention. I don't particularly like them very much, but they have had one of the leading roles in this book so it's only right to spare them a thought.

So what about my voices? What were they? Who were they? Well I'm still unsure as to the answers to these questions, but there's one thing I'm convinced of. And that is, you can't just put them down to an illness. I mean, they're voices for pity's sake: voices spoken in a language that I understand. Even if my mind did create them, I feel it is shallow and unfair just to label this as an illness. I mean, what other illnesses know how to talk?

The voices must mean something, and one thing in my case that I did notice, was that the voices' mood would generally fluctuate depending on my actions at the time, or with whatever it might be that was currently on my mind. If I did something bad – the voices would tell me off; something good – they would congratulate me.

So, maybe in my case, it was actually my conscience speaking out silently inside me, which you could say has resulted in me becoming a better person.

However, this does not mean to say that I ever deserved a life-sentence of mental illness in any way, shape or form: my very own, personal, Black Friday; sitting at the front of the cinema, paranoid and scared. But there's something that I have come to understand. Black Friday doesn't have to be a life sentence. Haven't you ever heard of happy Mondays?

There's seven days in the week and sure enough, Friday will be round again. So when it arrives, hear this – stay away from the lemonade and don't let Friday ever be black. There are many brighter colors, all far superior to the dull and draining and soul-destroying shades of black. There might even be a pot of gold at the end of the rainbow, but in the darkness of black you will just get lost. Trust me – I know.

I am aware that for some people who suffer from a mental illness, a solution might not be easy to find, so all I can say to this is – keep trying.

For me, the support from my friends and family, and finally my injection programme, was enough for me to wake up one morning and realize it was Saturday.

Like I said, I will probably receive my injections for the rest of my life, but, to be honest, I would rather that be the case than ever have to go through my ordeal again. In fact, now I would be scared to stop taking my injections because I know just how much they have helped me to get better.

So you see, it's not all doom and gloom. Every cloud does potentially have a silver lining, and hopefully this book has somehow, in a way, kind of proved this to be so.

Ah... yes... this book. Well... maybe this would be a good time to enlighten you with a few more facts, Jack.

You see, for all that time when I was ill, I felt that I was living in a world where people were monitoring me and sometimes trying to harm me for some reason. But I know now that this was not the case. Nobody wanted to hurt me really. Why would they?

So really, from the point where I moved away from Croydon, up until when I finally started to take my injections properly, I spent a large chunk of this time living in a reality that was delusional. It wasn't real.

And guess what? Well, I said to you earlier that this book, strictly speaking, is not an autobiography, and that's because a large chunk of this book is delusional too. It isn't real.

Yes, it's true that I was hearing voices and thought people were monitoring me. Yes, it's also true that I went to the hospital to get an x-ray. But guess what. There was nothing there at all! No tracking-device of course, but that's right – no pin either.

Oh come on, you didn't really think that I'd been walking around with a pin in my hip for ten years, did you? Well, I've got to say it – that's just mental!

And my voices weren't trying to warn me about my block of flats collapsing because, the truth is, they didn't collapse at all! As far as I'm aware, the block is still standing and the landlord is probably as mean as ever.

And did you really believe that a police dog ate one of my tablets? Come on – that's just mental!

And if I did really find a gold ring belonging to my fiancée – no sorry – girlfriend, do you honestly believe I would propose to her with it whilst she's giving birth? Don't be silly – that's just mental!

Yes, Marcus did have a leaving party before he joined the Army, but it wasn't at *Dibdabs* – there is no such place. Nor is there a chocolate shop in Shrewsbury called *Cacao Loco* (bloody good name for one though). But yes, there is a bookstall in the market, and my dear old dad does run this stall, but there's no way he would leave me in charge for the day – especially on *National Book Day*.

Ah yes – *National Book Day*. Is there such a thing? Well we seem to have National Pretty Much Anything Day, so I would imagine so, but I haven't got a clue if we do, or when it is, nevertheless.

And no, Toby didn't really grill a boiled egg and then become a head chef. And Marcus didn't really smash some geezer's legs with a bowling ball either. Bloody hell, Eric would have gone mental if he did!

The list goes on. Do you honestly believe that I would steal chicken skewers off the Turks when they have got razor-sharp kebab knives at their disposal? Oh, hang on a minute I do recall actually doing that once upon a time. Sugar – I must be mental!

Oh yeah, Mum really does cook this liver and bacon casserole which is truly shocking. I know it's a good idea to get a bit of iron in your body Mum, but a whole piece of it doesn't count!

Forget about the casserole and you should get my point. Basically, this whole book is just a made-up, complex, plot – not to destroy your world or to harm you, but just to show you how easy it can be to believe something that isn't true.

The clue was in the title. I said in the introduction that it is foolish to judge a book by its cover, but that is exactly how you should have judged this book. It is quite simply one big 'mental note' from start to finish.

Maybe I'm wrong. Maybe it was obvious that this book is bogus. I suppose it doesn't really matter: I just hope you enjoyed it. I certainly enjoyed writing it. I guess it's an example of how your imagination really can set you free.

And that's the end of it. It's not a happy ending: it's not a sad ending. It's just an ending. But what do they say about endings? New beginnings, I guess.

**EPILOGUE**

*Eric's wedding speech*

*I told you near the beginning about Eric's wedding speech. It was absolutely disastrous, but I feel that it would be unfair not to include it in this work. He created such an intense and electrifying atmosphere, that, at one point, I nearly choked on a piece of pork.*
*So – take it away Eric, my son (sorry – step-dad):*

"Thank you, thank you. Firstly, I'd like to thank all of you for coming here today, to join Stella and myself on this glorious occasion. The weather's pretty rotten though, don't you think? I look around and I recognise about five of you, so that's great isn't it? Stella's obviously got a lot more friends than me, but that's okay – I'm sure that you're all really nice people. You better had be anyway, because this damned wedding's cost me an arm and a bloody leg, but never mind hey, she's worth it I suppose. Anyway the older I'm getting – the less fussy I can afford to be, and I know just how lucky Stella feels to land me so I couldn't disappoint her could I? Anyway Stella you look great I have to say. Not quite as good as me though. I got this green little number tailor-made, which really does complement my highly distinguished physique – you lucky girl. Anyway for those of you who don't know me, I would just like to get one thing straight. I have never worn lady's underwear – ever! I have never roamed around the streets in a pair of suspenders and high-heels despite the rumours okay – that's rubbish! Anyway I don't want to talk about it anymore, I'm sick of it. I'll tell you one thing though, when I do find out who started those rumours there's going to be hell to pay. I am going to find out who did you know, and when I do there's going to be bloody murder! If it was any of you then you can just get out right now. Go on – GET OUT!

Anyway I don't want to talk about it anymore so just forget about it okay, I'm sorry. Right then – onwards and upwards. Now – I see marriage pretty much the same as buying a second-hand car. Firstly, you want to know how many miles it's done. Secondly, you want to know what state the engine's in, so you have a look under the bonnet: if that all seems to be satisfactory, then you need to find out if it runs properly, so you take it for a test drive. I've been test-driving Stella for years, only to find out recently that she runs on bloody diesel. No wonder she's a bit cranky. Anyway I've decided that she's not a bad little runner – should pass the MOT. Anyway, if you're happy with everything and you've got a good deal, then comes the contract, which is why we are all gathered here today – to sign the paperwork. Now then: I would just like to say that I'm quite happy with things the way they are at the moment. I'd like to quote something that you've all probably heard before: any two people can buy a house, but it takes two very special people to make a home. That's probably why we are having a few problems with that one. I'm happy with things the way they are at home, that lampshade looks good on that table. Then I would come into the room to find that she's put it somewhere else completely. Next she'll say she wants the 'magnolia' instead of the 'oatmeal' walls, which I only decorated a month ago. Never mind, it's her house. I wish her bloody son would move out soon though. He just doesn't pull his finger out enough. He even expects me to do the dishes every night, in fact, are you here Will? Oh there you are, I'll be talking to you afterwards, okay sonny? Right then,

where was I? I would like to
say that I'm not completely
happy with the food. Your
cake doesn't look too bad I
suppose Christine, thanks.
But did anyone find any
bones in their fish? They've
got stuck in my teeth and I
can't seem to get the
damned things out. It's okay,
I'll be having a word with the
manager later on, don't you
worry about that. Fish
bones? On my wedding day?
I don't think so, pal. Anyway,
you lot can't complain, you're
not paying for it are you?
Right, I've nearly finished,
think I've covered everything
anyway. I would just like to
say one more thing though,
and that is: Stella, I love you.
I will always look after you, till
one of us is dead, I can
promise you that. Any
arguments we might have in
the future, I want you to know
now that you win. Willy –
hurry up and get a job
please, I'm not even joking.
Okay that's it, so if you will all
please raise your glasses
and join me in a toast. Come
on – raise your glasses –
now please...Can you bunch
of sad sacks just raise your
bloody glasses please!
Thank you. To me and
Stella, the dashing groom
and his very lucky bride."

It was nearly the shortest wedding on record.

And Mum thought I had problems!

+

Proverbs and Definitions

"The mind is its own place, and in it self
Can make a Heav'n of Hell, a Hell of Heav'n."
John Milton – Paradise Lost

www.ingramcontent.com/pod-product-compliance
Lightning Source LLC
Chambersburg PA
CBHW031202270326
41931CB00006B/374